Baudelaire is a libertine, mystical, 'satanic,' but, above all, Wagnerian.

— Nietzsche

Baudelaire epitomizes the metaphysics of the provocateur.

— Walter Benjamin

Mon cœur mis à nu

La question (torture) est, comme art de
découvrir la Vérité, une niaiserie barbare,
c'est l'application d'un moyen matériel
à un but spirituel.

La peine de Mort est le résultat d'une
idée mystique, totalement incomprise aujourd'hui.
La peine de Mort n'a pas pour but de
sauver la Société, matériellement du moins. Elle
a pour but de sauver (spirituellement) la Société
et le coupable. Pour que le Sacrifice soit parfait,
il faut qu'il y ait assentiment et joie de
la part de la victime. Donner du Chloroforme
à un condamné à mort serait une impiété,
car ce serait lui enlever la conscience de sa
grandeur comme victime et lui supprimer les
chances de gagner le Paradis.

Quant à la torture, elle est née de la
partie infâme du cœur de l'homme assoiffé
de voluptés. Cruauté et volupté, sensations
identiques, comme l'extrême chaud et
l'extrême froid.

Charles Baudelaire

MY HEART LAID BARE
& other texts

Translated by
Rainer J. Hanshe

Contra Mundum Press   New York · London · Melbourne

Translation of *Mon cœur mis à nu*,
and Introduction © 2017 & 2020
Rainer J. Hanshe

First Contra Mundum Press
Edition 2017; 2nd printing, 2020.

All Rights Reserved under
International & Pan-American
Copyright Conventions.
No part of this book may be
reproduced in any form or by
any electronic means, including
information storage and retrieval
systems, without permission in
writing from the publisher,
except by a reviewer who may
quote brief passages in a review.

Library of Congress
Cataloguing-in-Publication Data
Baudelaire, Charles, 1821–1867
[*Mon cœur mis à nu*. English.]
My Heart Laid Bare & Other
Texts / Charles Baudelaire;
translated from the French by
Rainer J. Hanshe

—1st Contra Mundum Press
Edition
280 pp., 5 × 8 in.

ISBN 9781940625218

   I. Baudelaire, Charles.
  II. Title.
 III. Hanshe, Rainer J.
  IV. Translator.
   V. Introduction.

2017931985

TABLE OF CONTENTS

  0   STRANGE BEAUTY: THE DEFORMED ŒUVRE
       Introduction by Rainer J. Hanshe

  0   CHOICE OF CONSOLING MAXIMS ON LOVE

 12 AUTOBIOGRAPHICAL NOTE
 16 FLARES
 66 MY HEART LAID BARE
156 HYGIENE · CONDUCT · METHOD · MORALITY
170 Precious Notes
172 [Thoughts & Aphorisms]

178 NOVELLAS & NOVELS

184 FRAGMENTS & NOTES

192 THE PHILOSOPHER OWL

198 DRAWINGS

218 A NOTE ON THIS EDITION

Why should the poet not be a grinder of poisons as well as a confectioner, not raise serpents for miracles and performances, a psylle in love with his reptiles, and enraptured by the icy caresses of their coils at the same time as by the terrors of the crowd?

— Baudelaire, from a letter to Jules Janin

I want to vent my anger in terrifying books. I want to turn the whole human race against me. The pleasure this would give me would console me for everything.

— Baudelaire, from a letter to his mother

STRANGE BEAUTY: THE DEFORMED ŒUVRE[1]

To my Venus

> "I am very much at ease under my *stigmatization*, and I
> *know* that from now on, in whatever kind of literature
> I radiate, I shall remain a monster and a werewolf."
> — Letter to Victor Hugo

The title *My Heart Laid Bare* is Edgar Allan Poe's, and it is he who conceives of a book that, if daring enough, if 'bare' enough, could revolutionize human thought, opinion, and sentiment. This could be achieved, Poe said, "by writing and publishing a very little book. Its title should be simple — a few plain words — 'My Heart Laid Bare.' But this little book must be true to its title." Baudelaire took up Poe's provocation and his *Mon cœur mis à nu* is one of a number of different books that he dreamt up & hoped to write "without lassitude — in a word to be in good heart day after day."[2] Others Baudelaire mentioned in an 1864 letter included *Histoires grotesques et sérieuses*, *Les fleurs du Mal* (expanded), *Le Spleen de Paris*, *Les paradis artificiels*, *Contemporaines*, and *Pauvre Belgium!* The first notes for *Mon cœur mis à nu* begin in 1859, two years after the initial publication of *The flowers of Evil*, if not possibly somewhat earlier, and continue until 1865, ceasing only due to Baudelaire's severe health condition (he would die in 1867 at just 46 years of age), hence they comprise the final decade of his writing life.

Aside from the more direct root of Poe, Rousseau was another of Baudelaire's models, albeit a negative one to surpass. Baudelaire said that "all the targets of [his] rage" would be collected in *Mon cœur mis à nu*. "Ah! if ever that sees the light of day, J-J's *Confessions* will seem pale." *My Heart Laid Bare* is not however some memoir-like spewing of Baudelaire's *bios*; rather, it is the baring of his *esprit*, and as a crystallization of such, it isn't some kind of tell-all exposé (Rousseau's notion of absolute transparency, an indulgence we could well do without, especially considering its pernicious ramifications), but a much higher form of 'confession.' As an apodictic work of aphorism, maxim, note, and extended reflection, it is the arc of thought, the play of a mind in its every breadth that is bared. It contains Baudelaire's exhortations on work, faith, religion, and politics, excoriating sociological analyses, diatribes on literature (George Sand receives some choice malicious arrows), the arts, love (women, prostitution, sadomasochism, erotics *en générale*), and adumbrations of his conceptions of the Dandy and the Poet.

In 1861, two years after beginning *Mon cœur mis à nu*, sieged by resignation, calumny, and ill health (nervous disorders, vomiting, insomnia, fainting fits, recurrent syphilitic outbreaks), Baudelaire expresses doubt that he will ever complete his various projects. "My situation as regards my honor, frightful — and that's the greatest evil. Never any rest. Insults, outrages, affronts you can't imagine, which corrupt the imagination and paralyze it."[3] Three years later, it was against the continuing extremities of an exacerbated solitude, frayed nerves, self-described terrors, and constant hounding by creditors that Baudelaire implored himself to remain stalwart ("I must pull myself together, take heart! This may well bring rewards.")[4] and write.

Clearly, Baudelaire did envision publishing *My Heart Laid Bare* in his lifetime, and he diligently worked at it, steeling himself against his trials to the degree within his power, but it was never finalized. The obstructions he faced were abundant, the somatic afflictions inordinately taxing. The threat of his impending decline or decay is sharply articulated in one passage wherein he speaks of "feeling the wind of the wing of imbecility" passing over him.[5] His aphasia and heart attacks led to his losing his ability to speak, and thereafter, his ability to read and write — the death of the writer.

We have then only the existing fragments, which have been translated in full, but they were published posthumously. Despite no such title existing in the text, or any related material, French editors originally published the work as "Journaux intime" (Intimate Journals), which included two other sections, "Fusées" and "Hygiène." Translations into English followed suit, and the false title was adopted. It must at last be discarded. If Baudelaire hadn't been besieged by illnesses as he was, he would have imaginarily given us a definitive version of *Mon cœur mis à nu*, especially considering that he did complete other books he began around the same period (*Le spleen de Paris*, *Les paradis artificiels*, et cetera). It is an incomplete & fragmentary work then, yet one that is substantive enough to merit our continued attention.

In his poet's notebook, Paul Valéry said that "a work is never necessarily *finished*, for he who has made it is never complete, and the power and agility he has drawn from it confer on him just the power to improve it [...]. *He draws from it what is needed to efface and remake it.* That is how a *free* artist, at least, should regard things."[6] Similarly, he says elsewhere that, "in the eyes of lovers of anxiety and perfection, a work is never *finished* but *abandoned*."[7] Since Baudelaire never prepared a definitive version of *Mon cœur mis à nu*, we cannot know what he would have changed, or not, yet as a work closely aligned with his self, it's something that could never have been completed, only abandoned. Hence, it would always remain fragmentary, but such is to be differentiated from that which has not been finely honed. Consider Schlegel's poetics of the fragment, where even 'incompleteness' is exceptionally refined, an architecturally precise aesthetic form (sculpturally, such calls to mind Giacometti). In his essay on German Romanticism, Walter Benjamin pointed out that aphoristic writing is not proof against systematic intentions (an accurate insight he made about Nietzsche's work in fact, albeit one lost on many of the philosopher's later readers), that one can write aphoristically and still think through one's philosophy or writing "in a comprehensive and unitary manner in keeping with one's guiding ideas."[8] In that way, it is not that Baudelaire's book lacks cohesiveness; it is deliberately fragmentary to eschew finality, & because the self, the 'heart' being laid bare, is never complete, and can never be complete. That Baudelaire worked on the book for nearly ten years makes it probable that its character was quite well defined before illness permanently disrupted his being able to voluntarily abandon it.

Within the fragmentary mosaic of *My Heart Laid Bare*, there are unities, or thoughts that overlap and intertwine, similar extremities and intensities which are pursued, as there are with other books of Baudelaire's, including parts of his work on Belgium, *Pauvre Belgique* (*Poor Belgium*), or *La Belgique déshabillée* (*Belgium Stripped Bare*) as he later renamed that largely misunderstood diabolic satire on Belgium, France, and America.⁹ Like that incendiary work, this too is a work of *correspondance*, though in far less oblique ways. To speak of fires, what, one might ask, is "Flares" (in French, "Fusées")? Quite simply, it is a writer's notebook; as such, it doesn't have a single focus, but is more motley, something of a hybrid entity. To paraphrase, we could call it The Poet Laid Bare (of poetic form). Nonetheless, it has two principal nerve centers: *critique* and *meditation*.

The critique is many-tendrilled, with its points of observation being the craft of the writer, art and aesthetics, love, pleasure, and intoxication (numerous types), religion and theology, politics, etc. The writer's smelting room and sometimes place of furious venting. As with *Mon cœur mis à nu*, there is a root in Poe, who in his *Marginalia* spoke of "a peculiar type of criticism" that "can only be designated by the 'German 'Schwärmerei' — not exactly 'humbug' but 'sky-rocketing'…"¹⁰ Baudelaire took up Poe's arrow, naming his work "Fusées," an expansive translation of the English skyrockets. A *fusée* is a pyrotechnical device (rocket, flare, or firework), musket, or heraldic emblem, hence the title corresponds well with the work's variegated character. It is something incendiary and combative, yet elegant. The manifold subtitles peppered throughout "Flares" offer us a provisional overview of its character, too:

Plans, Projects, Suggestions, Notes, Hygiene, Morality, Conduct, Method. Here we see the writer's notebook, the critique, the meditation.

In speaking of intellectual gymnastics, the altar of the will, moral dynamics, the great deed, perfect health, the hygiene of the soul, political harmony of character, eurhythmy of character and faculties, self-purification, mastery of time, and accomplishing duties, Baudelaire enumerates a compendium of terms and concepts related to self-cultivation. The book thus contains a kind of technology of the self, an outline of Baudelaire's martial praxis for the artist — intellectual gymnastics and the sanctification of the will both bespeak an agonistic sensibility, as does his paean to greatness and his call to achieve it in contradistinction to the tremendous oppositional force of nothing less than an entire nation. What is this but Baudelaire's Miltonic-Satanic typology: "The man of letters rends foundations…" ("Flares" §6). Such terminology, and his repeated invocations to himself to master his will and to work diligently to become who he is, are part of a regimen of poetic self-shaping: "*Want every day to be the greatest of men!!!*" (MHLB §70) The references to Emerson and his *Conduct of Life* (cited in English in the original) further reinforce this, making for but one reason why in the synopsis to this book a parallel is made to Marcus Aurelius, characterizing *My Heart Laid Bare* as Baudelaire's meditations. The poet is clearly concerned with self-government, and this shaping or cultivation of the self is meant to strengthen the poet, thereby aiding his accomplishing his artistic tasks, of which the book is in part a record.

Those notions can be woven together with other parts of the work, i.e. §16 of "Flares," where Baudelaire speaks of the most perfect type of virile Beauty (the Miltonic Satan), or the Emersonian hero (he who is immovably centered), giving us the supreme artistic model of Satan, that is, Satan as the light-bringer, a visionary, he who is anti-human ("Let us defy the people, common sense, the heart, inspiration, & evidence" (§47); too: "The man of letters is the enemy of the world" (§53)). In §21 of "Flares," Baudelaire asks, "To give oneself to Satan, what is it?" This book provides us with some answers, as does his poetry (the "Litanies of Satan" *et alia*), and his Dandy (a superior figure) is another type with similarly sublime aspirations. It is the onset of the anti-Christian *hyperanthropos*. "The poet, the priest, and the soldier are the only great men among men: ... the rest are made for the whip" (MHLB §47).

To consider Baudelaire's notion of the Dandy and Dandyism, a brief typology of such can be constructed through examining some of the passages wherein he refers to both, not only within *My Heart Laid Bare*, but within his œuvre. In "Dandyism," an essay in *The Painter of Modern Life*, Baudelaire describes Dandyism as a social attitude as strange as dueling, an exilic institution, a form of self-invention, a cult of the ego, a form of self-government, a spiritual or philosophical praxis, and a form of heroism in the midst of a decadent age. The Dandy is also an enemy of democracy. Baudelaire roots the figure socio-politically, diagnosing that it is a type born during a limbic stage "when democracy is not yet all powerful and aristocracy is only just beginning to totter and fall."[11]

In its simplest form, the Dandy is one who makes his life into a work of art, which begs the question, what is a work of art to Baudelaire? He has clearly definite ideas of that, but to elaborate upon them here would take us into another labyrinth. Let each reader make it a pursuit.

In *My Heart Laid Bare*, Baudelaire speaks of the Dandy as one who "must aspire to be sublime without interruption; he must live & sleep before a mirror" (§5), which is a key passage on the Dandy. Beyond cultivating a refined appearance (which begs another question: *what is appearance and what does it signify?*) and suggesting a possibly self-enclosed reality, that statement (declaration?) can also refer to self-reflection, to the ceaseless act of learning to know oneself and becoming who one is, just as it suggests dreaming before a reflective optical object, therefore, to *projecting* one's dreams, visions, etc. to the world (the very work of creation).

Yet, is a mirror only strictly a literal mirror, or are other things (objects, people, animals, etc.) mirrors before which the dandy lives & sleeps as well? If the world is a mirror and the dandy lives & sleeps before it, is he not one who is *contra mundum*, one who stands in opposition to what most value as meaningful? Recall Baudelaire's gibe about usefulness: — to be useful is *hideous* (a damning of mercantile and bourgeois values, of the protestant work ethic, so beloved by America's status quo). And when the poet proclaims that Dandyism is "an institution outside the law,"[12] it evokes his statement about the man of letters being "an enemy of the world" (MHLB §53). Yet the Dandy also "has a rigorous code of laws,"[13] hence he is not lawless, only free of the world's laws (and morals). While Foucault admired if not adopted Baudelaire's concept of the Dandy, in his essay on the Enlightenment the philosopher noted that "'the doctrine of elegance' imposes 'upon its ambitious and humble disciples' a discipline more despotic than the most terrible religions."[14] While judgment of that can be left to each individual reader, think of §12 in "Flares" wherein Baudelaire says that "the true saint is the one who whips and kills the people for the good of the people." Could we paraphrase: "The true Dandy is the one who whips and kills himself for the good of himself"? Is what Foucault calls despotism not then but a fierce martial regimen for self-overcoming (in my analogy, the flagellation and annihilation are not meant literally) in order to achieve sublimity? *"Above all*, TO BE *a great man* and *a Saint* for oneself" (MHLB §42). One passage Baudelaire cites from Emerson's *Conduct of Life* is here apposite: "Great men... have not been boasters and buffoons, but perceivers of *the terror of life*, and have manned themselves to face it."[15] The martial praxis I spoke of earlier is thus not a fanciful or errant interpretation. While Baudelaire had an antagonistic relationship to his father-in-law General Aupick, even once supposedly attempting to have him assassinated, he seems to have been marked by his regimental character, but cultivated it as a drive for perfecting his poetics.

To return to the Dandy's task of developing a refined appearance, consider this caveat from *The Painter of Modern Life*: "Dandyism is not even an excessive delight in clothes and material elegance. For the perfect dandy, those things are no more

than the symbol of the aristocratic superiority of his mind."
Conceivably, such is what Nietzsche meant in part when he
spoke of the profundity of superficiality — the surface is
made into a spectral projection of the interior (the depths);
the inner world and its every dimension become a panoply
of scintillating folds rippling on the surface of a body. Think
of reality being a hologram of the cosmos. And by negative
definition, the Dandy is anti-natural and highly refined: in *My
Heart Laid Bare*, Baudelaire states that "Woman is the opposite of the Dandy" because she "is *natural*, that is, abominable,"
and so "always vulgar, that is, the opposite of the Dandy" (§5).
This seems to imply that woman is *a natural dandy* therefore,
according to Baudelaire, she cannot be a true Dandy. In *The
Painter of Modern Life*, a parallel is also made between Dandyism and "spirituality and stoicism," whose gymnastic exercises
are meant "to strengthen the will and school the soul"[16] (Dandyism as dueling).

Baudelaire is clearly not some lackadaisical café rat devoid
of great drives and satisfied with the weakest form of pulsions.
The Surrealist dream that everyone becomes a poet (adopted from Lautréamont) would probably — *rightfully* — be a
nightmare to him, indicative of what he saw as the leveling
spirit of democracy. "Can you imagine a Dandy speaking to
the people, except to scorn them?" (MHLB §22) Baudelaire
was far more exacting in his poetics and compared the Dandy's doctrine of elegance and originality to "the most rigorous
monastic rule," akin to "the inexorable commands of the Old
Man of the Mountain."[17] The Dandy could be conceived of

as a kind of poetic samurai — not only a warrior, but a highly refined person, a practitioner of the arts, a hopeful master of *bunbu-ryōdō* (the two ways of the civil and martial arts). Ultimately, for Baudelaire, the Dandy is a figure of opposition and revolt and "representative of what is best in human pride, of that need to combat and destroy triviality."[18] Camus argued that the Dandy's existence is only found "in the expression of others' faces" (a mirror) and that "he plays at life because he is unable to live it."[19] This is contestable. Rather, it is an ecstatic life, lived at the highest pitch, an exilic life of limit experiences and extreme expenditure.

When equating women with the natural world, Baudelaire declares them "abominable" and states that they cannot be Dandies. For many *contemporary* readers (and contemporaneity is not modernity), always reading with temporary attentiveness and *out of tempo*, that is, *ahistorically*, questions of misogyny naturally arise. To pursue the absolute logical extreme of where this arrow could lead, let us paraphrase the title of a famous book on Sade and here ask, for it is the temper of the time, *Must We Burn Baudelaire?* Undoubtedly, *le poète maudit* is not an advocate of equality, and therefore not someone to seek political guidance from. Walter Benjamin said that, "Ultimately, Baudelaire's political insights do not go fundamentally beyond those of professional conspirators."[20] He had contempt for humanity in general, despised most artists and writers, saw only poets, priests, and warriors as venerable, avowed that all love is prostitution, *&* declared God the most prostituted being. Is his caustic view of women different then from any of those barbs and declarations, or his caustic view of the human species itself? And is this a matter of personal prejudice or, conversely, a matter of the ruling mores of the time, which he perhaps didn't always escape? To address this thorn, just as with the Dandy *et alia*, requires examining all of the passages wherein Baudelaire speaks of women before being able to come to a more complete, and thereby just, understanding of his views, unless we want to succumb to facile denunciations (a predominant propensity of this censorious and vindictive decade). In *Baudelaire's Prose Poems*, Edward Kaplan noted that Baudelaire's practice easily surpasses our theories. In lieu of an impossible totality, a few observations.

To focus on the passage just referred to, its context concerns a question about what is natural, and it is precisely naturalism in relation to Dandyism that Baudelaire is critical of. If something is innate, then there can be no art, for there is no invention, no act of transfiguration. Nonetheless, Baudelaire's view of women being natural Dandies could be contested. If artifice or Dandyism is natural to women, then every woman would be a master of such, which is not the case. How many Claude Cahuns are there? Baudelaire doesn't seem to recognize, at least in the passage in question, that artifice is learned, cultivated, developed; what is seemingly natural becomes such through a long period of incorporation and practice. Artifice is a discipline. Baudelaire's viewpoint is also specific to a culture and a civilization, in particular to a period when women's lives were severely circumscribed and their place in socio-political spheres virtually non-existent, save for rare cases, like that of

Lou Andreas-Salomé. But what would Baudelaire think of the males of the African Wodaabe tribe, who do more to cultivate their beauty than the female Wodaabes? Since the men are trained from youth in the art of artifice, could they be true Dandies? And what of many 18th-C European men, who from their youth onward powdered their faces, rouged their cheeks and lips, and wore wigs — according to Baudelaire's perspective, would not both be considered abominable?

To reflect on another passage, consider the dedication to *Les paradis artificiels*, where Baudelaire says that "woman is the being who projects the greatest shadow or the greatest light into our dreams. Woman is fatally suggestive; she leads another life in addition to her own; she lives spiritually in the imaginations she haunts & fertilizes." Julia Kristeva observes that there is an ambivalent splitting here toward amatory objects that are both ideal and abject.[21] Yet, since Baudelaire equates the artist with the prostitute, whenever he speaks of the prostitute, he could also be speaking of the artist (and/or poet), which makes for a further splitting or ambivalence. The prostitute in Baudelaire's work is both a member of the polis (a literal prostitute), and a concept or type (the artist). What too are we to make of the fact that, in *Paradis artificiels*, Baudelaire disguises himself as a curious, mature woman with an excitable spirit?

To present a definitive counter view of (supposed) Baudelairean misogyny, in his poem on Sappho, Baudelaire describes the ancient Greek poet as virile, recognizing in her the same quality of strength he recognizes in his Miltonic Satan, and speaks of admiringly. Simply writing of lesbian erotics in France in the mid-18th C was, if not an anomaly, certainly far from common. And Baudelaire's poetry is peopled with lesbians, prostitutes, courtesans, old women, and widows; they are not excluded from his urban reality, but compose a large part of it. One of the reasons why the original edition of *Les fleurs du Mal* was in part banned was due to the poems about lesbians. Baudelaire saw beyond the object of desire and focused on desire itself as a pulsional force, free of all moral tenor. He was fined 300 francs for offending public morality and forced to suppress numerous poems from *Les fleurs du Mal* to gain permission to publish the book. The country of *liberté, égalité,* and *fraternité* was not so emancipated, hardly amoral, far from it. It wasn't until 1944 that women were granted suffrage in France, and not until as late as 1975 that abortion was legal there — so much for enlightenment in the city of lights. In freely writing about lesbians and seeing their desire as no different from the desire of Don Juan, Baudelaire didn't suffer from the moral priggishness that prevailed in the Second Empire, and which continued into the 20th C, and still in many ways prevails today. To the horror of one of his landlords, Baudelaire also had a black lover. But naturalism, now *that's* abominable. It seems quite solemn and sacrosanct not to see how that is rather comical, but this age is largely humorless.

In the poem "The Ideal," we also have another definitive counter view of supposed Baudelairean misogyny. Baudelaire overturns the predominant stereotype of his time of women as anemic and weak and sings the praises of Lady Macbeth, and of the figure of Night, one of Michelangelo's magisterial sculptures of a strong, vigorous woman, a figure who starkly contrasts any conventional notion of woman as gentle, passive, and obedient. Night is a Titan. Ultimately, it is the cogitating, powerful, self-directed Lady Macbeth, a figure whose heart is abyssal in its depth and who embraces her desires, that Baudelaire expresses admiration for, extols as an ideal.

The women scorned in some passages cannot therefore be women in general, but only a certain type of woman (the constricted role women were limited to at that time, hence hardly an expansive state of becoming), a gender trait many women themselves reject. In fact, in his early essay on Poe, Baudelaire argues that the reason why many writers regard women as nothing but household utensils or objects of lust (his words) is due to their not having received an adequate political and literary education. It is a brief passage, but he recognizes that differences between men and women are not in any degree due to character or essence, but to women having been largely ostracized from the socio-political sphere. In the same essay, he also criticizes his beloved Poe for being quite anti-feminine. Finally, to look briefly at a poem we can relate to the question of naturalism, in "Confession," the poem's female narrator avows that the work of being a beautiful woman is not only difficult, but banal and mechanical, which seems to in fact cancel or negate the viewpoint that Dandyism is natural to women. If not, it certainly complicates the statement.

Let us also consider, in brief, a drawing: the self-portrait of a young Baudelaire on page 212 of this book — recently discovered and published here in the US for the first time. It contains what may be the poet's only nude drawing, which seems to be a loving, gentle depiction of one woman performing cunnilingus upon another (& pinching her nipple), who is gazing directly at us, free, comfortable, devoid of any shame, and joyful. It's not a very fine drawing, hardly comparable to Baudelaire's self-portraits, but it does convey (as his other drawings of women) a distinctly different sentiment than some of the poems about women, yet perhaps it is a self-portrait too, of Baudelaire disguised as a woman, a corollary to his disguised female presence in *Paradis artificiels*.

Whatever the case, we see here how passages from a notebook cannot be too easily seized upon and taken as definitive and representative 'viewpoints.' While undoubtedly embodying aspects of the misogyny particular to the time period, ultimately, a more nuanced, complex, and variegated or *tensional* view of women exists in Baudelaire's œuvre. And what more incandescent and volcanic performance of Baudelaire do we have than Diamanda Galas' *Litanies of Satan*? Clearly, Baudelaire's views of women didn't impede Galas from reading or working with him, and she brooks no fools. Today, Sade is still read, and he will continue to be read tomorrow, and the same will be true of Baudelaire. If perfectly ethical viewpoints (from what perspective?) are to dictate our reading, a host of books would have to be dispensed with, or, far worse, *burnt*, which would be to engage in upholding social 'purity' through the cleansing (or destruction) of what is 'degenerate,' a fascistic pursuit, even if limited to censorship, for censorship is a form of silencing and silencing is a subtle form of death, of ostracization.

What now of the Dandy? Is there a contemporary corollary of Baudelaire's uncompromising insurgent? If the Dandy was a type that, according to Baudelaire, was born during an interstice between the supremacy of democracy and the decay of aristocracy, then no. It is beyond the will of the subject — the political phenomenon that generates such a mutinous figure doesn't exist. However, if we want to consider the perspective of a populist magazine, then, as Nick Carvell argues in his fluff piece "What is a Modern Dandy,"[22] Dandyism does exist, and a capitalist pop star is but one embodiment of it, which is difficult to consider with anything but derision. *Dandyism as populism??* Baudelaire's dandy would speak to "the people" only to scorn them, whereas the pop star in question struts before yet supplicates the publicum, desperately yearning to be worshipped. Carvell's conception of the Dandy is attenuated and frivolous, limited mostly to haberdashery and opposing dress standards, where style alone is a form of self-fashioning. In that, the surface is not a reflection of a depth, but strictly a surface, or an attitudinal pose. To Baudelaire, the delight in clothes and material elegance are no more than symbols of the aristocratic superiority of the Dandy's mind. There is clearly no such superiority of mind in Carvell's article, let alone in his subjects, including those in the videos accompanying the article. They evoke more what the French in the 19th C., including Baudelaire, called *gandins*, an untranslatable word, though perhaps it is akin to a fop. *Gandins* were elegant young men, more or less ridiculous, who frequented the boulevards during the Second Empire, obsessed as they were with appearance and with always 'being seen' in the 'right places.' The term was popularized via Paul Gandin, a character in Theodore Barrières play, *Les parisiens* (1855). At that time, it was linked etymologically to Boulevard de Gand (now Boulevard des Italiens), a meeting place for those who considered themselves elegant. It wasn't one of Baudelaire's haunts. The *gandins* surely would have been astonished by his having a black lover. In *La curée*, Zola refers to them as pigs and imbeciles. What these figures are evidence of is not Dandyism, but conformism, or the 'culture' of capitalism.

To Carvell, being a Dandy is "all about playing with what we consider traditional masculinity," which is nothing less than a corrosion of Dandyism, the diminishing of something formerly incandescent and nefarious to a withering husk of itself. Since longstanding forms of identity have basically been eroded, is there even any such thing as traditional masculinity? Carvell also restricts Dandyism to men, and elsewhere in his piece speaks of living in a period of less restrictive dress codes, which thereby makes "dressing a little more on the dandy side" "ever easier." This perspective makes Dandyism sound simply like an act of posing and accessorizing. Dandy today, punk tomorrow, frivolous forever. To Sebastian Horsley, being a Dandy was about being adored (his own declaration). Hence, ease — acceptability *&* veneration, conformism essentially, hardly revolt — is part of the makeup of *the contemporary Dandy*. Is that even remotely akin to Baudelaire's

Dandy, or to Beau Brummel, or to Oscar Wilde and Jean Genet, or Bowie's Ziggy Stardust, who played with androgyny long before *gender-bending* became popular and accepted? If the GQ notion of the Dandy entails in part a cult of the ego and some form of self-invention, it is hardly an exilic institution, let alone a form of self-government on the scale of what Baudelaire envisioned. Is there in such people (Carvell's list) a *ceaseless* act of self-knowledge? Would any of them be capable of writing a book as searching and Marsyan as Wilde's *De Profundis*? And do they possess a parallel with spirituality and stoicism as rigorous as what Baudelaire imagined? And are they enemies of democracy, or figures of opposition and revolt (in more than merely facile, sophomoric ways)? They seem to mostly be advocates and devotees of capitalism, consumers waiting, *hoping*, to be consumed. In contrast to the frivolous leniency that largely prevails today, let's opt against accepting some severely diminished form of Dandyism, sustain a higher, more rigorous standard of valuation, and not let Dandyism be annexed, neutered, and deformed into something akin to instant pudding. All of that may sound severe or restrictive to the indulgent, who seem to equate freedom with the total abjuration of any standard of value, but remember that Camus proclaimed Baudelaire to be "the most profound theoretician of dandyism."[23] To abandon all standards of value is to suffer from a poisonous aspect of democracy, to descend into a realm where everything is permitted because nothing is true, a problematic even Nietzsche found troubling, not cause for celebration.[24]

What one might wonder would Baudelaire think of certain contemporary public figures? To push this beyond a possible mere animus of his, what is at work in his critiques is a criterion of value that is rooted to a diagnostic view of culture and civilization. To refer to his remarks as a symptomatology à la Nietzsche might be overstated, for, generally, Baudelaire does seem to be speaking directly about whichever object of his spleen, whereas whomever Nietzsche 'attacks' in his agons, he also values and admires, as befits a thinker who has shattered simple dichotomies.[25] Despite the above caveat about Baudelaire, we could nonetheless interpret his criticisms similarly. For example, take what he says in *My Heart Laid Bare* of George Sand and her lack of belief in hell and read it alongside what he says of her in his notes on De Laclos' *Les liaisons dangereuses*: "In reality, Satanism has won. Satan has made himself innocent. Evil that is conscious of itself is less frightful and closer to healing than evil that is ignorant of itself. G. Sand inferior to Sade."[26] Here we have a theological critique of evil & our consciousness of it. For Baudelaire, to see nature in Rousseau's terms as innocent, as Sand does, is to lack knowledge, to be ignorant of the existence of evil, or not to offer any alternative reasoning or logic for it (as Nietzsche would later, and Freud), whereas Sade is conscious of it, and because of that, he is superior, and the knowledge he imparts to us about evil is of greater value, which thereby makes his writing of greater value. As Baudelaire says in his cahiers, "We must always return to Sade, that is, to *the Natural Man*, to explain evil."[27]

To enumerate the subjects of Baudelaire's symptomatology then: style and whether it is eternal or not; individual versus herd mentality; flowing style as negative; the anti-artist and strict materialist (Voltaire is the representative type here); drunken inferior pedantics (the principle negative qualities of the literary rabble); the avant-garde as non-militant conformists who can only think as crowds; democracy as the enemy of art; the relationship between sexuality, art, and potency, etc. That is a list of mostly negative, not positive types (or, subjects & some representatives of their types), but some of the positive ones were enumerated earlier. In a letter to his mother, Baudelaire diagnoses the Parisians to be a decadent race, and one that he is so horrified by, it makes him want to flee humanity altogether:

> You have no idea how much the Parisian race has declined. [...] artists know nothing, authors know nothing — not even how to spell. All these people have become abject, perhaps inferior to common folk..... — I want to flee from the face of humanity, but especially from the face of the French.[28]

Considering that, what might Baudelaire think of our age?? Imaginably, we could engage in a thought experiment and exchange the names in the following jeremiad of his with ones from our own time to determine his possible diagnosis:

> With the exception of Chateaubriand, Balzac, Stendhal, Merimee, de Vigny, Flaubert, Banville, Gautier,

> Leconte de L'Isle, all the modern riffraff horrifies me. Virtue, horror. Vice, horror. A fluent style, horror. Progress, horror. Never talk to me anymore about those who say nothing.[29]

Leave it to each reader to conclude who of our time would be an exception for Baudelaire, and who would horrify him. Fluent style (easily digestible prose) alone would bring down a whole wealth of writers, the near-entirety that is of those whom many people admire and extol as 'great,' and who are the object of focus in most print & media sources today. We hear their names again and again, ad nauseam. But if someone were to now write the kind of critique that Baudelaire did in his time, all the self-appointed judges would come out of the woodwork with their sickles & scarlet letters.

Where readers might ask does *My Heart Laid Bare* fit (or not) into Baudelaire's œuvre? There is a passage in "Flares" wherein Baudelaire transmogrifies the nature of beauty, declaring that its essential and characteristic element is that which is slightly deformed, a disproportion that includes irregularity, the unexpected, surprise, astonishment. What isn't slightly deformed, he says, is lacking in sensitivity, which is a subtle but incisive damnation of a classical precept, also a focus of attack in his final essay on Poe. That transfigured, affirmative notion of beauty as deformity is emblematic not only of *My Heart Laid Bare*, but of Baudelaire's œuvre itself. It's an anamorphosis of classical aesthetics, and thereby an ushering into being of true modern aesthetics — Baudelaire gives birth to, or *forges*, a new, transgressive definition of beauty.

A similar declaration exists in his essay "The Universal Exhibition of 1855": "*The beautiful is always bizarre.*" In writing of marginal and extreme characters such as dandies, criminals, whores, beggars, lesbians, and other similar outcasts, or to use Nazi terminology, what would be considered *Entartete* (degenerate) material, Baudelaire enacted a transvaluation of the classical canon and what constitutes the adjudicated 'content' of art, putting it into metamorphosis. To concentrate on such material and make it the province of art, the focus of that about which one is sensitive and which warrants representation or focus — and Baudelaire was a seismograph of such material —, is to transfigure art itself. To crack apart a restrictive, suffocating aspect of the classics — what is outdated of tradition — and jettison us into modernity. Although he recognized Baudelaire's genius, T. S. Eliot essentially ridiculed his "stock of imagery," stating that Baudelaire's "prostitutes, mulattoes, Jewesses, serpents, cats, corpses, form a machinery which has not worn very well,"[30] but this critique is warped and ignorant. What Eliot neglects to discern (or was too orthodox to countenance, too conservative, too moralistic, at least in this assessment) is that Baudelaire was inaugurating an aesthetic that stands in strict contradistinction to any notions of purity, heroism, supreme health, physical perfection, etc., which we could retrospectively deem an antifascist aesthetic.

To write a book called *Les fleurs du Mal* was both a subversive critical *&* creative act. In his late essay on Poe, Baudelaire points out that the phrase "decadent literature" is academic and denounces the classicists for their focus on morality of purpose and merit of intentions as loci of critique. Such he declares is part of the maelstrom of mediocrity, and that same maelstrom blusters about us now, to the nth degree, in nefarious and vicious ways. *Le poète maudite* was one of the principal figures to have established, and vindicated, an aesthetics of ugliness (the dreadful, the fearful, the morally offensive, the *ill-shaped*, from the Greek *dyseides*, Latin *deformis* (think here of being de-formis, that is, *beyond genre* (without clearly defined form) and the principles of genre), Sanskrit *ku-rupa*), locating beauty in the strange, the castoff, the calamitous, the disdained. A striking example of his celebration of such is his prose poem "In Praise of Dogs":

> Retreat Academic Muse! I've no use for such an old prude. I invoke the familiar muse, the urbanite, the lively one, to help me to sing of good dogs, of poor dogs, of despicable dogs, of those whom everyone kicks away as plague-stricken and poisonous, except the poor whose brethren they are, and the poet who looks upon them with a fraternal eye.
>
> Fie upon the fop dog, fie upon the fatuous Danish quadruped, the King Charles, the pug or rascal, so enchanted with itself that it leaps indiscreetly against the legs or on a visitor's lap, as if desperate to please, boisterous as a child, foolish as a harlot, sometimes snarling and insolent like a servant! Fie especially upon those four-pawed serpents, shivering and indolent, which are called greyhounds, and which don't even have in their pointed muzzles enough flair

to follow the trail of a friend, nor in their flattened heads enough intelligence to play dominoes!

Back to the kennel, all such tiresome parasites! Let them return to their silky and padded kennels!

I praise the despicable dog, the poor dog, the homeless dog, the roaming dog, the saltimbanque dog, the dog whose instinct, like that of the poor, the gypsy, and the stage actor, is wonderfully sharpened by necessity, that very good mother, that true patroness of intellects!

I praise the calamitous dogs, those who wander, lonely, in the sinuous ditches of great cities, or those who with their winking and spiritual eyes have said to forsaken men: 'Take me with you, and with our two miseries, perhaps we shall create a kind of happiness!'[31]

The Nazi's notion of the degenerate was based partly upon Nordau's book *Entartung* (*Degeneration*), and Baudelaire was one of its key subjects, for his life demonstrated to Nordau all the mental *stigmata* of degeneration. In using such rhetoric in his etiology, Nordau essentially made Baudelaire into a martyr, and when describing his death and the aftermath of his acolytes, he made an analogy between Baudelaire and Alexander the Great and his generals, further endowing his heritage with a stately, heroic aura, though that wasn't Nordau's aim. He focused on numerous poems from *Les fleurs du Mal* to illustrate that *le poète maudite* was attracted to what Nordau defined as the morbid, criminal, and lewd, while even Baudelaire's fear of abysses (*cremnophobia*) betrayed "the obsession of a diseased mind." Nordau also referred to Verlaine as "a repulsive degenerate subject with an asymmetric skull and Mongolian face, an impulsive vagabond & dipsomaniac." I would not be sharing salt or spirits with Nordau, or any of his ilk, any time. Give me the vagabonds and dipsomaniacs. Let us sit at table with Rabelais. Baudelaire's poetics of deformity endowed 'abnormality' with dignity, and clearly triumphed over Nordau's *moraline* critique — *le poète maudite* became one of the incandescent beacons of the 20th century, while Nordau has the Nazis as bedfellows. *My Heart Laid Bare* concentrates (and exalts) Baudelaire's transmogrified notion of *strange beauty*; it is a fragmentary and aphoristic equivalent of the poetry, prose poems, and essays, their critical-creative corollary. The work of one who is anti-human (the stigmatized monster & werewolf). A flower of Evil.

Like Nietzsche, Baudelaire was a posthumous writer far in advance of his time, which he was wholly aware of, and stated: "I have some convictions, in a higher sense, and which cannot be understood by the people of my time" (MHLB §11). Now, exactly a century-and-a-half after his death, Baudelaire's convictions have proven to carry his work into the future and make it an object of continued fascination. *Le poète maudite* was not only disruptive, shocking, and scandalous in his lifetime, but, if we don't allow our clichés and certainties to efface him and his texts, he will remain ever so demanding and disruptive. A figure of strange beauty.

ENDNOTES

1. This introduction is a revised version of answers I provided to Edwin Turner when he interviewed me in March and April of 2017 for his site *Biblioklept*. The passages on translation and on Baudelaire's drawings have been almost entirely excised. The interview was published on May 1, 2017.
2. Baudelaire, *Selected Letters: The Conquest of Solitude* (1986) 211.
3. Ibid., 161. Letter to his mother, May 6, 1861.
4. Ibid., 211. Letter to his mother, 1865.
5. Other translators have rendered that phrase as "the wing of madness," but Baudelaire says "*imbécillité*," not *folie* or *démence*. The notion of "the wing of madness" has greater Gothico-Romantic cache, but it's not what Baudelaire says, and in this case, there's a relatively exact equivalence of terms between French and English. It was more physical weakness and feebleness that Baudelaire feared, and experienced, and believed would finally incapacitate him, as it did, *not* madness.
6. Paul Valéry, *The Art of Poetry* (1958) 177–78.
7. Ibid., 140–41.
8. Walter Benjamin, *Selected Writings: 1913–1926* (1996) 136.
9. For an in-depth analysis of the book, see the introduction to my translation of *Belgium Stripped Bare* (2019).
10. Edgar Allan Poe, *Complete Works, Vol. III* (1949) 493, §XV.
11. Baudelaire, *Selected Writings on Art and Artists* (1981) 421.
12. Ibid., 419.
13. Ibid.
14. Michel Foucault, "What is Enlightenment," *The Foucault Reader* (1984) 48.

15. Ralph Waldo Emerson, *The Conduct of Life* (2003) 2. Cited by CB in §93B of "Flares" and "Hygiene."
16. 421.
17. Ibid.
18. Ibid.
19. Albert Camus, *The Rebel* (2012) 52.
20. Walter Benjamin, *The Writer of Modern Life: Essays on Charles Baudelaire* (2006) 48.
21. Julia Kristeva, *Tales of Love* (1987) 331.
22. Nick Carvell, "The Modern Dandy," *GQ* (October 10, 2016). Online: www.gq-magazine.co.uk/article/the-modern-dandy
23. Camus, op. cit., 53.
24. When Zarathustra's Shadow avows (amongst a host of other things) that "nothing is true, everything is permitted," Zarathustra responds to it mournfully, stating that the Shadow has lost its goal (Nietzsche, *Thus Spoke Zarathustra*, "The Shadow"). For other passages where Nietzsche uses the phrase, see KSA 11: 88, 146, and *On the Genealogy of Morals*, Part III §24.
25. For Nietzsche, the 'enemy' is also always or simultaneously a 'friend,' and *vice-versa*. Whatever figure he chooses to criticize or, more affectively, 'attack' in his agons, is not a subject but a *typus* emblematic of a cultural, psychological, spiritual, or other phenomenon that demands critical scrutiny. What he attacks or criticizes, he respects as something *victorious* that has contributed to the shaping of culture, whether negatively or positively. As strong a critic as Nietzsche was of Socrates, he did say that Socrates was very close to him, which is one of the reasons why he had to continually fight him.

26. Baudelaire, "Notes analytiques et critiques sur *Les liaisons dangereuses*," *Œuvres posthumes* (1908) 409.
27. Ibid. Incidentally, Baudelaire does speak more positively of Sand in his early essay on Poe.
28. Baudelaire, *Correspondance* (2000) 279. Letter to his mother, August 10, 1862.
29. Ibid.
30. T. S. Eliot, *Selected Essays* (2014) 340.
31. My translation.

CHOICE OF CONSOLING MAXIMS ON LOVE

Whoever writes maxims likes to fortify his character; — the young powder themselves, — the old adonise themselves.

The world, this vast system of contradictions, — having all caducity in great esteem, — quickly, let us blacken our wrinkles; — feeling being quite customary, let us beribbon our hearts like a frontispiece.

To what good? — If you are not true men, be true beasts. Be naive, and you will necessarily be useful or pleasurable to some. — My heart, — even if set to the right, — will well find a thousand co-pariahs among the three billion beings who graze the nettles of feeling!

If I begin with love, it is because love is for everyone, — though they may deny it, — the great thing of life!

———

All of you who feed some insatiable vulture, — you Hoffmannesque poets whom the harmonica sets dancing in crystal regions, and whom the violin lacerates like a blade that seeks the heart, — bitter and gluttonous contemplators to whom the spectacle of nature itself gives dangerous ecstasies, — that love be to you a sedative.

Tranquil poets, — *objective* poets, — noble partisans of method, — architects of style, — politicians who have a daily task to accomplish, — that love be to you a stimulant, a fortifying and tonic beverage, and the gymnastics of pleasure a perpetual encouragement to action!

To these here soporifics, to those there alcohols.

You for whom nature is cruel *&* time precious, that love be an animate and burning cordial to you.

One must therefore choose one's loves.

Without denying *love at first sight*, which is impossible, — see Stendhal, *On Love*, book I, chapter XXIII, — one must believe that fatality enjoys a certain elasticity, which is called human freedom.

Just as for theologians, liberty consists in avoiding opportunities for temptation rather than resisting them, so, in love, freedom consists in avoiding the categories of dangerous women, that is, dangerous for yourself.

Your mistress, the woman of your heaven, will be sufficiently indicated to you by your natural sympathies, verified by Lavater, by painting, and by statuary.

The physiognomic signs would be infallible, if we knew them all, and well. I cannot here give all the physiognomic signs of women who are eternally suitable to this or that man. Perhaps one day I will accomplish this enormous task in a book entitled *The Catechism of the Beloved Woman*; but I am certain that each man, aided by his imperious and vague sympathies, and guided by observation, can find in a given time the necessary woman.

Besides, our sympathies are generally not dangerous; nature, in cooking as in love, rarely gives us a taste of what is bad for us.

As I hear the word "love" in the fullest sense, I am obliged to express some particular maxims on delicate questions.

A Man of the North, an ardent navigator lost in fogs, a seeker of auroræ borealis more beautiful than sunlight, indefatigable thirster of the ideal, loves cold women. — Loves them well, because the labor is greater and more bitter, and you will find one day more honor at the tribunal of Love, which sits beyond the blue of the infinite!

A Man of the South, whose open nature has no taste for secrets *&* mysteries — frivolous man, — of Bordeaux, Marseille, or of Italy, — ardent women will suffice for you; this movement and this animation are your natural empire; — amusing empire.

Young man, you who wish to be a great poet, guard yourself against the paradox in love; let schoolboys drunk on their first pipe sing at the top of their voices the praises of the fat woman; abandon those lies to the neophytes of the pseudo-romantic school. If the fat woman is sometimes a charming caprice, the skinny woman is a well of dark delights!

Never slander great nature, *&* if she has awarded you a mistress without breasts, say: "I have a friend — with hips!" and go to the temple to render thanks to the gods.

Know how to take advantage of ugliness itself; of your own, it is too easy; all the world knows that Trenk, *the Burning Maw*, was worshiped by women;[1] of *hers!* that is more rare and more beautiful, but the *association of ideas* renders it easy *&* natural. — I postulate your sick idol. Her beauty has disappeared under the frightful crust of smallpox, as verdure under the heavy ices of winter. Still moved by the long agonies *&* fluctuations of illness, you contemplate with sadness the ineffaceable stigmata upon the body of the beloved convalescent; you suddenly hear resonate in your ears a *dying* air, executed by the delirious bow of Paganini, and this sympathetic air speaks to you of yourself, and seems to tell you the entire poem of your lost inner hopes. — From then on, the traces of smallpox will be part of your happiness, and beneath your sensitized gaze the mysterious air of Paganini will always sing. Henceforth, they will not only be the objects of gentle sympathy, but also of physical rapture, if you are one of those sensitive spirits for whom beauty is above all the *promise* of happiness. It is, therefore, the association of ideas above all that makes the ugly beloved; because, if your pockmarked mistress betrays you, you will greatly risk being able to console yourself only with pockmarked women.

For certain more curious and more blasé spirits, the rapture of ugliness arises from an even more mysterious feeling, which is the thirst for the unknown, and the taste for the horrible. It is this feeling, of which each carries within himself

---

1. We could have quoted Mirabeau, but this is very common, and besides, we suspect that he was sanguine ugly, which is particularly antipathetic to us. [Baudelaire's note. Hereafter, any notes by CB himself are cited: [CBN].]

the germ, more or less developed, which precipitates certain poets into clinics & dissecting rooms, & women into public executions. I would vigorously lament those who cannot understand; — a harp that lacks a bass string!

As for spelling mistakes, which for some dimwits is part of moral ugliness, is it not superfluous to explain to you how it can be a whole naive poem of memories and raptures? The charming Alcibiades stuttered so well, and childhood has such divine gibberings! Beware then, young adept of rapture, of teaching French to your friend, — unless you must be her French teacher in order to become her lover.

There are people who blush for having loved a woman the day they realize that she is ferine. They are vain Aliborons, made to grind the most impure thistles of creation, or enjoy the favors of a bluestocking. Atavism is often the ornament of beauty; it is this that gives the eyes the mournful limpidity of dusky ponds, and the oily calmness of tropical seas. Atavism always preserves beauty; it removes wrinkles; it is a divine cosmetic that preserves our idols from the sting of thought that we must suffer, hideous savants that we are!

There are some who do not want their mistresses to be prodigals. They are Holy Asses, or republicans who are ignorant of the first principles of political economy. The vices of a great nation are its greatest wealth.

Others, the supine, reasonable, and moderate deists, the just-milieu of dogma, who are enraged at seeing their women throw themselves into devotion. — Oh! the clumsy, who can never play any instrument! Oh! the triple fools who do not see that the most adorable form religion can take, — is that of their wife! — A husband to convert, what a delicious apple! The beautiful forbidden fruit that a great impiety, — in a tumultuous winter night with fire, wine, and truffles, — a mute canticle of domestic happiness, a victory won over rigorous nature, which itself seems to blaspheme the Gods!

I should not have finished too soon, if I wanted to enumerate all the beautiful & good sides of what is called vice and moral ugliness; but a difficult and anguished case often presents itself, to people of heart and intelligence, as a tragedy; it is when they are caught between the hereditary and paternal taste of morality and the tyrannical taste of a woman whom they ought to despise. Numerous & ignoble infidelities, the habits of places of ill-repute, shameful secrets wrongly discovered, inspire you with horror for the idol, and sometimes your joy gives you a shudder. You are very much impeded in your Platonic reasonings. Virtue and pride cry out to you: Flee it! Nature says in your ear: Where to flee? Terrible alternatives where even the strongest souls reveal all the insufficiency of our philosophical education. The most adroit, seeing themselves constrained by nature to play the eternal novel of Manon Lescaut & of Leone Leoni? have become unhinged in saying that contempt goes very well with love. — I will give you a very simple recipe that will not only free you of these shameful justifications, but also enable you not to bruise your idol, & not to damage your *crystallization*.[2]

---

2. We know that all of our readers have read the *Stendhal*. [CBN]

I suppose that the heroine of your heart, having abused the *fas* and the *nefas*, has arrived at the limits of perdition, after having — final infidelity, supreme torture! — tried the power of her charms on her jailers and executioners.[3] Will you abjure the ideal so easily, or if, faithful and weeping, nature precipitates you in the arms of this pale victim of the guillotine, will you say with the mortified accent of resignation: Contempt & love are first cousins! — Not at all, for those are the paradoxes of a timorous soul and an obscure intelligence. — Say boldly, and with the candor of the true philosopher: "Less defiled, my ideal would not have been complete. I contemplate her, and submit myself; of such a powerful rascal, great Nature alone knows what it wants to make of her. Supreme happiness & reason! absolute! *resulting* from contraries! Ormuz and Arimane, you are the same!"

And it's thus, thanks to a more synthetic view of things, that admiration will naturally lead you back to pure love, that sun whose intensity absorbs all spots.

Remember this, it is especially the paradox in love that we must guard against. It's naiveté that saves; it's naiveté that rends happy, though your mistress be as ugly as old Mab, the queen of terrors! In general, for the people of the world, — a clever moralist has said it, — love is only the love of gambling, the love of fighting. It is a great wrong; love must be love; fighting and gambling are only permitted as the politics of love.

---

3. As well as [Jules Janin's] *L'Âne mort* [*et la femme guillotinée*]. [CBN]

The most serious error of modern youth is that of *forcing their emotions*. A good number of lovers are imaginary invalids who spend a great deal on pharmacopoeias, and pay M. Fleurant and M. Purgon handsomely, without having the pleasures and privileges of a genuine illness. Note well how they enervate their stomachs with absurd drugs, and exhaust in themselves the digestive faculty of love.

Although it is necessary to be of one's century, be careful not to ape the illustrious Don Juan, who at first was nothing but, according to Molière, a rude rascal, well styled *&* affiliated with love, crime, and quibbles; — then became, thanks to M. Alfred de Musset and Théophile Gautier, an *artistic* flâneur, running after perfection through places of ill-repute, and finally was no more than an old dandy exhausted by all his travels, and the stupidest of the world to an honest woman well-disposed to her husband.

Summary and general rule: in love, beware of the *moon* and the *stars*, beware of the Venus de Milo, of lakes, guitars, rope ladders, and all novels, — the most beautiful in the world, — even if written by Apollo himself!

But love well, vigorously, gallantly, orientally, ferociously the one that you love; so that your love, — harmony being well understood, — does not torment the love of another; that your choice does not disturb the state. Among the Incas one loved his sister; be content with your cousin. Never climb balconies, never insult public power; don't deprive your mistress the sweetness of believing in Gods, and when you accompany her to the temple, know how to properly dip your fingers in the pure and fresh water of the stoup.

———

All morals attesting to the good will of the legislators, — all religion being a supreme consolation to all the afflicted, — every woman being a piece of the *essential* woman, — love being the sole thing worth writing a sonnet and dressing in fine linen for — I revere these things more than anything else, and I denounce as a calumniator whoever makes this scrap of morality an occasion for the sign of the cross and food for scandal. — Glittering morality, is that not it? Colored glass tinting perhaps too brightly the eternal lamp of truth that shines within? — Not at all, not at all. — If I had wished to prove that everything is for the best in the best of all possible worlds, the reader would have the right to say to me, as to the *ape of genius*: you are a wicked man! But I wanted to prove that everything is for the best in the worst of all possible worlds. It will then be much forgiven me, because I loved very much ... my male ... or my female reader.

[AUTOBIOGRAPHICAL NOTE]

Childhood: Old Louis XVI furniture, antiques, consulate, pastels, eighteenth-century society.

After 1830, the college of Lyon, coups, battles with professors and comrades, severe melancholy.

Return to Paris, college & education by my father-in-law (General Aupick).

Youth: Expulsion from Louis the Great, episode of the baccalauréat.

Travels with my father-in-law in the Pyrenees.

Free life in Paris, first literary connections: Ourliac, Gérard, Balzac, Levavasseur, Delatouche.

Travel in India: first adventure, dismasted ship; Mauritius, Île Bourbon, Malabar, Ceylan, Indoustan, Cap; happy walks.

Second adventure: return on a ship without food & sinking.

Return to Paris; second literary connections: Sainte-Beuve, Hugo, Gautier, Esquiros.

Difficulty for a very long time of making myself understood by the editor of any newspaper.

Permanent taste since childhood for all plastic representations.

Simultaneous interests in philosophy & beauty in prose & in poetry; of the perpetual, simultaneous relationship of the ideal with life.

FLARES

1
FLARES

Even if God did not exist, Religion would still be Holy and *Divine*.

God is the sole being who, to reign, does not even need to exist.

That which is created with the mind is more alive than matter.

Love is the taste for prostitution. There is not even one noble pleasure that cannot be reduced to Prostitution.

At a show, at a ball, everyone is enraptured by all.

What is art? Prostitution.

The pleasure of being in crowds is a mysterious expression of the rapture of the multiplication of number.

All is number. Number is in *all*. Number is in the individual. Intoxication is a number.

The taste for productive concentration ought to replace, in a mature man, the taste for degradation.

Love can be derived from a generous feeling: the taste for prostitution; but it is soon corrupted by the taste for property.

Love wants to abandon itself, to confound itself with its victim, as the conqueror with the vanquished, & yet preserve the privileges of the conqueror.

The raptures of one who maintains a woman are due to both the angel and the owner. Charity and ferocity. They are even independent of sex, of beauty, & of animal kind.

The green shadows in the humid evenings of the beautiful season.

Great depth of thought in vulgar phrases, hollowed out by generations of ants.

Anecdote about the hunter, related to the intimate connection between ferocity & love.

2

FLARES

Of the femininity of the Church, as the reason for its omnipotence.

Of the color violet (love restrained, mysterious, veiled, color of a canoness).

The priest is great because he makes the horde believe in a multitude of astonishing things.

That the Church wants to make everything and every being is a [necessity] law of the human spirit.

People worship authority.

Priests are the servants and sectaries of the imagination.

The throne & the altar, a revolutionary maxim.

E.G. or the SEDUCTIVE ADVENTURESS

Religious intoxication of the great cities. — Pantheism. I is all; All is I.

Whirlwind.

3
FLARES

I believe that I have already written in my notes that love has a strong resemblance to an act of torture or to a surgical operation. But this idea can be developed in the most bitter manner. Even if two lovers enamor one another very much and are full of reciprocal desires, one of them will always be calmer or less possessed than the other. He or she is the surgeon or the executioner; the other is the subject, the victim. Do you hear those sighs, the preludes of a tragedy of dishonor, those groans, those cries, those rales? Who has not uttered them, who has not irresistibly extorted them? And what baser thing find you than the question administered by conscientious torturers? Those contorted somnambulist eyes, the limbs of which the muscles twitch and stiffen as if under the action of a galvanic battery, — drunkenness, delirium, and opium, in their most furious results, will certainly not give you cases as [beautiful] frightful, [and] also as curious. And the human face, which Ovid believed was fashioned to reflect the stars, speaks [reflects] here only of an expression of mad ferocity, or relaxing into a type of death. For, indeed, I should believe it would be sacrilege to apply the word ecstasy to this sort of decomposition.

— Dreadful game where one of the players must lose the government of him or her self!

In my presence someone once asked what the greatest pleasure of love consisted of. Someone naturally answered: to receive, — and another: to give oneself. — The former said: the pleasure of pride! — and the latter: the rapture of humility! All those foul-tongues spoke like the *Imitation of Jesus Christ*. — Finally, an impudent utopian was found who affirmed that the greatest pleasure of love consisted of creating citizens for the country.

Myself, I say: the unique and supreme rapture of love [consists] rests in the certainty of doing *evil*. — And man and woman know [then] from birth that in evil [we find] is found all rapture.

4
PLANS · FLARES · PROJECTS

— The Comedy à la Silvestre.
  Barbara and the Sheep.
— Chenavard has created a superhuman type.
— My vow to Levaillant.
— Preface, mixture of mysticalness & playfulness.
  Dreams and Dream Theory in Swedenborg.

The thought of Campbell (*The Conduct of Life*).
Concentration.
The power of a dominant idea.
— Absolute frankness, a means of originality.
— Pompously recount comic things.

5
FLARES · SUGGESTIONS

When a man takes to bed, nearly all his friends have a secret desire to see him die; some to verify that his health is inferior to theirs; others in the disinterested hope of studying an agony.

The arabesque is the most spiritualist of designs.

6

FLARES · SUGGESTIONS

The man of letters rends foundations and conveys a taste for intellectual gymnastics.

The arabesque is the most ideal of all designs.

We love women in proportion to their being [strangers] strangers to us. To love intelligent women is a pleasure of the pederast. Thus bestiality excludes pederasty.

The spirit of buffoonery need not exclude charity, but it is rare.

Enthusiasm applied to something other than abstractions is a sign of weakness & disease.

Thinness is more naked, more indecent than corpulence.

7

— *Tragic heaven*. Epithet of an abstract order applied to a material entity.

— Man drinks light with the atmosphere. Thus the populace is right to say that night air is unhealthy for work.

— People are born fire worshippers.
Fireworks, conflagrations, incendiaries.
If we imagine a born [, a Parsi] fire worshipper, a [Pars] *born Parsi*, we could create a novella.

8

Mistakes concerning [people] faces are the result of an eclipse of the real image by the hallucination born of it.

Know then the raptures of a harsh life; and pray, pray without ceasing. Prayer is a reservoir of strength. (*Altar of the Will. Moral Dynamic. Sorcery of Sacraments. Hygiene of the Soul.*)

Music hollows out the heavens.

Jean-Jacques said that he could not enter a cafe without a certain emotion. For a timid nature, the ticket-booth of a theater is somewhat akin to the tribunal of Hell.

Life has but one true charm; it is the charm of *Gambling*. But if we are indifferent to winning or losing?

9
SUGGESTIONS · FLARES

Nations have great men only in spite of themselves, — like families. They make every effort not to have one. And thus, to exist, the great man needs to possess a force of attack much greater than the force of resistance developed by millions of individuals.

About sleep, the sinister adventure of our every night, one can say that men daily fall asleep with an audacity that would be unintelligible if we did not know that it is the result of their ignorance of the danger.

10

There are some skins as hard as shells against which contempt is no longer a vengeance.

Many friends, many gloves. Those who loved me were despised, I might even say contemptible, if I wanted to flatter honest people.

Speak Latin, Girardin! *Pecudesque locutæ*.

To send Robert Houdin to the Arabs to divert them from miracles is the work of an incredulous Society.

11

Those great & beautiful ships, imperceptibly balanced (waddling) on tranquil waters, those robust ships, look idle and nostalgic as they ask us in a mute tongue: When do we set sail for happiness?

Not to forget the marvelous in drama, sorcery, & romance.

The background, the atmospheres in which a whole story must be tempered. (See "Usher" and refer to the profound sensations of hashish & opium.)

12

Are there mathematical follies and madmen who think that two and two make three? In other words, — can hallucination, if those words do not scream out [to be coupled], invade the things of pure reasoning? If, when a man becomes accustomed to sloth, dreams, and idleness, to the point of constantly deferring what is important till the morrow, another man awakened him one morning with terrible lashes, and whipped him ruthlessly until, being unable to work out of pleasure, he would work out of fear, would not this man — the whip-bearer — really be his friend, his benefactor? Besides, one could say that pleasure would come after, much more correctly than one says: love comes after marriage.

Similarly in politics, the true saint is the one who whips and kills the people for the good of the people.

Tuesday, May 13, 1856

Take some copies to Michel.

Write to Mann,
    to Willis,
    to *Maria Clemm*.

Send to Mad. Dumay
— know if Mirès...

What is not slightly deformed seems insensitive; — whence it follows that irregularity, that is, the unexpected, surprise, astonishment, are an essential and characteristic part of beauty.

13
NOTES · FLARES

Theodore de Banville is not precisely materialistic; he is luminous.

His poetry represents happy hours.

With each letter from a creditor, write fifty lines on an extra-terrestrial subject, and you will be saved.

A wide smile on the beautiful face of a giant.

14

Of suicide and suicide-madness considered in their relation to statistics, medicine, and philosophy.

Brière de Boismont

Look for the passage:
To live with someone who has nothing but aversion for you…
The portrait of *Sérène* by Seneca, that of *Stagyre* by St. John Chrysostom.
Acedia, the disease of monks.
The *Tædium vitæ*.

15
FLARES

Translation & paraphrase of: *The Passion relating everything to her*.

Spiritual and physical raptures caused by the storm, electricity, & lightning, tocsin of amorous, tenebrous memories, of distant years.

16

FLARES

I have found the definition of Beauty, — of my Beauty. It is something ardent and sad, something a bit vague, giving wing to conjecture. I will, if you like, apply my ideas to a sensitive object, to the object, for example, most interesting in society, to the face of a woman. A seductive and beautiful head, a woman's head, I say, is a head that makes one dream, at the same time, — but in a confused way, — of rapture and of sadness; which includes an idea of melancholy, of lassitude, even of satiety, — either an idea contrary, that is, to an ardor, a desire to live, associated with [a certain sadness] ebbing bitterness, stemming from privation or despair. Mystery, regret, are also characteristics of Beauty.

A beautiful male head has no need to convey, except perhaps in the eyes of a woman, — in the eyes of a man of course — this element of rapture, which in a woman's face [even the most melancholic] is a provocation all the more [enervating] attractive as the face is generally more melancholic. But that head will also contain something ardent and sad, — spiritual needs, darkly repressed ambitions — the idea of an unused, thundering power, — sometimes the idea of a vengeful insensitivity, (for the ideal type of the Dandy must not be neglected in this subject), — sometimes also, — and it is one of the most interesting characteristics of beauty, — mystery, and finally (so that I may have the courage to confess to what degree I feel modern in æsthetics), *Sadness*. — I do not pretend that Joy can not be associated with Beauty, but I say that Joy is one of the most vulgar [the least important] ornaments; — whereas Melancholy is, so to speak, [the illustrious companion] <[the natural companion]> <the illustrious companion>, to such an extent that I can hardly conceive (would my brain be a bewitched mirror?) of a type of Beauty where there is no *Sadness*. — Supported on, — others would say: obsessed with — these ideas, one can conceive that it would be difficult for me not to conclude that the most perfect type of virile Beauty is *Satan* — in the manner of Milton.

17

FLARES

Self-idolatry.

Political harmony of character.
Eurythmy of character & faculties.
Increase all faculties.
Preserve all faculties.
A cult (magism, evocative sorcery).
The sacrifice and the vow are supreme formulæ and symbols of exchange.

Two fundamental literary qualities: supernaturalism & irony.

[Turn of] The quick individual glance, the aspect [that is] in which things present themselves to the writer, then a satanic turn of spirit. The supernatural comprises the general color and the accent, that is, intensity, sonority, limpidity, vibrativity, depth, and tintinnabulation in space & time.

There are moments in life when time and expanse are more profound, and the feeling of life greatly increased.

Of magic applied to the evocation of the great dead, to the reestablishment and perfecting of health.

Inspiration always comes when a man *wants* it, but it does not always leave when he wants it to.

Of language & of writing, considered as magical operations, evocative sorcery.

Of the air in woman.

The charming airs & those that make beauty are:

The blasé air,	The imperious air,
The bored air,	The willful air,
The evanescent air,	The wicked air,
The impudent air,	The sickly air,
The cold air,	The feline, childish,
The air of looking within,	nonchalant, & mischievous air amalgamated.

In certain almost supernatural states [of the soul], the depth of life reveals itself entirely in the spectacle, however ordinary it may be, that one has before one's eyes. This becomes its symbol.

As I was crossing the boulevard, and as I was hastily moving to avoid the carriages, my halo broke off and fell into the mud of the macadam. Fortunately, I had time to pick it up; but the unhappy idea that it was a bad omen slipped into my mind a moment later; and from then on the idea would not let go of me; it left me no rest the entire day.

Of the worship of oneself in love, from the point of view of health, of hygiene, of grooming, of spiritual noblesse, and of eloquence.

Self-purification and anti-humanity.

There is in the act of love a great resemblance to torture, or to a surgical operation.

There is in prayer a magical operation. It is one of the great forces of the intellectual dynamic. It is like an electric recurrence.

The rosary is a medium, a vehicle; it is prayer put in the range of all.

Work, a progressive and accumulative force, bearing interest like capital, in faculties as in results.

Gambling, even guided by science, intermittent force, will be defeated, however fruitful it may be, by work, however slight it may be, but sustained.

If a poet asked the State for the right to have a few bourgeois in his stable, one would be very astonished, whereas if a bourgeois asked for some roast poet, it would be quite natural.

This book will not scandalize my women, my daughters, nor my sisters.

Sometimes he asked her permission to kiss her leg, and he took advantage of the circumstance to kiss that beautiful leg in such a position that it clearly etched her outline on the setting sun!

Pussy, muffy, muffilette, my cat, my wolf, my little monkey, big monkey, big serpent, my little melancholic ass.

Such caprices of language, too often repeated, too frequent bestial appellations, bear witness to a satanic side of love; do not satans have the forms of beasts? The camel of Cazotte, — camel, Devil, & woman.

A man goes to a shooting range, accompanied by his wife. — He selects a doll and says to his wife: I imagine that it is you. — He closes his eyes and slaughters the doll. — Then, he says, — ‹in kissing the hand of his companion›: Dear angel, I thank you for my skill!

When I have inspired universal disgust and horror, I shall have conquered solitude.

This book is not for my wives, daughters, or sisters. — I have few of those things.

There are shell-like skins with which contempt is no longer a pleasure.

Many friends, many gloves, — for fear of scabies.

Those who loved me were despised, I might even say contemptible, if I wanted to flatter *honest people*.

God is a scandal, — a scandal that returns.

18

FLARES

Do not despise anyone's sensibility. The sensibility of each person is his genius.

There are only two places where one pays to have the right to expend: public latrines and women.

By an ardent concubinage, one can imagine the raptures of a young household.

The precocious taste for women. I confused the odor of fur with the odor of a woman. I remember … Indeed, I loved my mother for her elegance. I was then a precocious dandy.

My ancestors, idiots or maniacs, in solemn apartments, all victims of terrible passions.

The Protestant countries lack two elements indispensable to the happiness of a well-bred man: gallantry and devotion.

The mixture of the grotesque and the tragic is as pleasing to the mind as dissonances to blasé ears.

What is intoxicating in bad taste is the aristocratic pleasure of displeasing.

Germany expresses dreams by the line, as England by perspective.

There is in the birth of all sublime thought a nervous jolt that makes itself felt in the cerebellum.

Spain puts the ferocity natural to love into its religion.

STYLE.

The eternal note, the eternal and cosmopolitan style. Chateaubriand, Alph. Rabbe, Edgar Poe.

19

FLARES

SUGGESTIONS

It's easy to imagine why Democrats don't like cats. The cat is beautiful; it evokes ideas of luxury, cleanliness, rapture, etc.

20

FLARES

A little work, repeated three hundred & sixty-five times, yields three hundred & sixty-five times a bit of money, that is, an enormous sum. At the same time, *glory is made*.

‹Likewise, a host of little pleasures make up happiness.›

Creating a stereotype is genius.
I must create a stereotype.

The concetto is a masterpiece.

The tone of Alphonse Rabbe.
The tone of the kept woman (*My beautiful everything! Fickle sex!*).
The *eternal* tone.
Rough coloring, deeply scored drawing.
The prima Donna and the butcher boy.

My mother is fantastic; she must be feared and pleased.

The haughty Hildebrand.
Cæsarism of Napoléon III. (Letter to Edgar Ney.) Father and Emperor.

21

FLARES · SUGGESTIONS

To give oneself to Satan, what is it?

What is more absurd than Progress, since man, as everyday fact proves, is always like & equal to man, that is, always in a savage state. What are the perils of the forest and the prairie in comparison to the daily shocks and conflicts of civilization? Whether man ensnares his dupe on the Boulevard, or pierces his prey in unknown forests, is he not eternal man, that is, the most perfect beast of prey?

— They say that I am thirty years old; but if I lived three minutes in one ... am I not ninety years old?

.... Work, is it not the salt that preserves the souls of mummies?

Start a novel, start a topic anywhere and, to have the desire to finish it, start with very beautiful sentences.

22

FLARES

I believe that the infinite and mysterious charm that lies in the contemplation of a ship, and especially of a ship in motion, is, in the former case, due to the regularity and symmetry that are one of the primordial needs of the human spirit, as much as complexity and harmony, — and, in the second case, from the successive multiplication and generation of all the curves and imaginary figures [described] operating in space through the real elements of the object.

The poetic idea that emerges from this operation of lines in motion is the hypothesis of a vast, immense, complicated, but eurythmic being, of a creature full of genius, suffering and sighing all human sighs and ambitions.

Civilized peoples, who always speak foolishly of *savages & of barbarians*, soon, as d'Aurevilly says, you will not *even be worth enough to be idolaters*.

Stoicism, a religion that has but one sacrament, — suicide!

Conceive a canvas for a lyrical or fairy buffoonery, for a pantomime, and translate that into a serious novel. To drown the whole in an abnormal and dreamy atmosphere, — in the atmosphere of *great days*. — That there is something soothing, — *&* even serene, in passion. — Regions of Pure Poetry.

Moved by contact with those raptures that resembled memories, sensitized by the thought of an ill-replete past, of many mistakes, of many quarrels, of many things to conceal from his lover, he began to weep; and his warm tears flowed into the shadow on the naked shoulder of his dear and still attractive mistress. She quivered; she too felt sensitized and moved. The shadows reassured the vanity and the dandyism of a cold woman. Those two fallen creatures, who still suffered from their remnant of nobility, embraced each other spontaneously, blending in the rain of their tears and kisses the sadnesses of their past with their highly uncertain hopes for the future. It is presumable that for them rapture had never been so sweet as on that night of melancholy and charity; — rapture saturated with pain *&* remorse.

Through the darkness of the night, he had looked behind himself into the deep of years, then he had thrown himself into the arms of his guilty lover to find there the forgiveness that she had granted him.

— Hugo thinks often of Prometheus. He applies an imaginary vulture to a breast that is only lanced by the [synapisms] *moxas* of vanity. Then the hallucination became complicated, varied, but according to the increasing progress described by the doctors, he believed that by a *fiat* of Providence, St. Helena had taken the place of Jersey.

This man is so hardly elegiac, so hardly ethereal, that he would horrify even a notary.

Hugo-Sacerdoce always has his forehead bent; — too bowed to see anything, except his navel.

What is not a priesthood today? — Youth itself is a priesthood, — according to youth.

And what is not a prayer? — Shitting is a prayer, what democrats say when they shit.

M. de Pontmartin, — a man who always seems to have arrived from his province…

Man, that is, each person, is so *naturally* depraved that he suffers less from universal abasement than from the establishment of a reasonable hierarchy.

The world will end. The only reason that it might endure is that it exists. How feeble this reason is, compared to all those who announce the contrary, particularly this one: what does the world henceforth have to do under heaven? — For, supposing that it continue to exist materially, would it be an existence worthy of the name & of the Historical Dictionary? I do not say that the world will be reduced to the expedients and grotesque disorder of the South American republics, — that perhaps we shall even revert to a savage state, and that we shall go, via the grassy ruins of our civilization, to seek our food, with rifle in hand. No; — for this fate and these adventures would still presuppose a certain vital energy, an echo of the earliest ages. New example, and new victims of inexorable moral laws, we will perish by way of that through which we believed we lived. The mechanical will have Americanized us so much, and progress will have so completely atrophied in us our entire spiritual character, that nothing among the sanguinary, sacrilegious, or anti-natural dreams of utopians can be compared to its positive results. I ask every thinking man to show me what remains of life. Of religion, I believe it useless to speak of it and to seek its remnants, since the trouble of denying God is the only scandal in such matters. Property had virtually disappeared with the abolition of the law of primogeniture; but the time will come when humanity, like an avenging ogre, will seize its last scrap from those who believe themselves to be the legitimate heirs of revolution. Still, that will not be the supreme evil.

The human imagination can conceive, without too much difficulty, republics or other communal states, worthy of some glory, if they are led by sacred men, by certain aristocrats. But it is not however through political institutions that universal ruin, or universal progress, will manifest itself; for the name [word] matters little to me. It will be by the abasement of hearts. Need I say that what little remains of politics will struggle painfully in the clutches of general animality, and that those who govern will be forced, in order to maintain themselves & to create a phantom of order, to resort to means that would make our present-day humanity, although so hardened, shudder? — Then, the son will flee the family, not at eighteen, but at twelve, emancipated by his gluttonous precocity; not to seek heroic adventures, not to free a beautiful prisoner from a tower, not to immortalize [to practice in a garret the sublime craft of writer] a garret through sublime thoughts, but to found a trade, to amass wealth, and to compete with his infamous papa, — founder and shareholder of a newspaper, which will spread enlightenment and which would make *Le Siècle* of the day seem to be an abettor of superstition. — Then, errant women, outcasts, those who have had several lovers, and who are sometimes [were once] called Angels, [because of bewildered passengers] in recognition *&* thankfulness for the thoughtlessness that illumines, [sometimes as the] light of luck, in their logical existence, like evil, — then they, I say, will be nothing but pitiless sages, sages that will condemn everything, apart from money, everything, even the *errors of the senses!* — Then, whatever resembles virtue, — said I, — whatever is not ardor for Plutus, will be deemed a great absurdity. Justice, if, at that fortunate period, it can still exist, will be prohibited to the citizens who cannot make a fortune. — Your wife, O Bourgeois! your [legitimate companion] chaste half, whose legitimacy seems poetry to you, now introducing into legality an irreproachable infamy, vigilant and loving guardian of thy strongbox, will no longer be the perfect ideal of the kept woman. Thy daughter, with [precocity] childish nubility, will dream in her cradle that she [will] sell herself for a million. And thou, O

Bourgeois, — less [poetic] poet than thou art today, — thou shalt find no fault with it; you will regret nothing. For there are things in man that strengthen and prosper in proportion as others become more delicate and decline, and, thanks to the progress of that age, nothing will remain of the entrails but viscera! — That age is perhaps very near; who knows if it has not already come, and if the coarsening of our nature is not the sole obstacle that prevents us from evaluating the environment in which we breathe!

As for myself, who sometimes senses within myself the ridiculousness of a prophet, I know that I will never find therein the charity of a physician. Lost in this villainous world, jostled by crowds, I am like a weary man whose eyes see behind him, in the deep years, only disillusionment ‹and bitterness›, & before him, only a storm that contains nothing new, neither knowledge, nor pain. The evening when this man has thieved [on the way] from destiny a few hours of pleasure, soothed by his digestion, oblivious — as far as possible — of the past, content with the present & resigned to the future, intoxicated by his sang-froid and his dandyism, proud of not being as base as those who pass by, he says to himself, while contemplating the smoke of his cigar: What does it matter to me where these consciences go?

I believe I have drifted into what people in the trade call an hors-d'œuvre. Nevertheless, I will leave these pages, — because I want to date my anger ‹sorrow›.

86

FLARES · HYGIENE · PROJECTS

"The more one wills, the better one wills."
The more one [wills] works, the better one works, and the more one wants to work. The more one produces, the more fertile one becomes.

After a debauchery, one always feels more alone, more abandoned.

Morally as physically, I have always had the sensation of the abyss, not only of the abyss of sleep, but the abyss of action, of dream, of memory, of desire, of regret, of remorse, of beauty, of number, etc.
I have cultivated my hysteria with rapture and terror. [Today] Now, I always have vertigo, and today, January 23, 1862, I have suffered a singular warning: I have felt the *wind of the wing of imbecility* pass over me.

87

HYGIENE · MORALITY

To Honfleur! as soon as possible, before falling further down.

How many presentiments and signs already sent by God, that it is *high time* to act, to regard the present minute as the most important of minutes, and to make a *perpetual rapture* of my ordinary torment, that is, of Work!

88

HYGIENE · CONDUCT · MORALITY

At every minute we are crushed by the idea and the sensation of time. And there are only two means of escaping this nightmare, — to forget it: Pleasure and Work. Pleasure consumes us. Work fortifies us. Let us choose.

The more we use one of these means, the more [we flee] the other inspires us with repugnance.

One can forget time only by using it.

[De Maistre & Edgar]

Everything is done little by little.

FLARES

De Maistre & Edgar Poe taught me to reason.

There is no long work but that which one dares not begin. It becomes a nightmare.

89
HYGIENE

By postponing what one has to do, one runs the risk of never being able to do it. By postponing conversion, one risks being damned.

To cure everything, misery, sickness, and melancholy, there is absolutely nothing but the *Taste of Work*.

90
PRECIOUS NOTES

Do every day what duty and prudence want.
If you work every day, life will be more bearable.
Work *six* days without relent.

To find subjects, γνῶθι σεαυτόν ... (List of my tastes).[4]

Always be a poet, even in prose. Grand style (nothing is more beautiful than the commonplace).

First begin, and then make use of logic *&* analysis. Every hypothesis wants its conclusion.

Find the daily frenzy.

---

4. The first Delphic imperative: Gnothi seauton (Know thyself).

91

HYGIENE · CONDUCT · MORALITY

TWO PARTS:

Debts (Ancelle).
Friends (*my mother, friends, myself*).
Thus, 1,000 francs must be divided into two parts of 500 francs each, and the second divided into *three* parts.

To Honfleur

Make a review and ranking of all my *letters* (2 days).
And all my debts (2 days). (Four categories: *banknotes, big debts, small debts, friends*).
Classification of engravings (2 days).
Ranking of notes (2 days).

92

HYGIENE · CONDUCT · METHOD

Jeanne 300, my mother 200, myself 300. 800 francs per month. To work from six in the morning, till noon, on an empty stomach. Working blindly, aimlessly, like a madman. We shall see the result.

I suppose I base my destiny on several hours of uninterrupted work.

Everything is reparable. There is still time. Who knows even if new pleasures…?

Glory, payment of my Debts. *Wealth* of Jeanne and of my mother.

I have not yet known the pleasure of a fulfilled plan. The power of obsession. The power of Hope.

The habit of accomplishing one's Duty dispels fear. One must want to dream and know how to dream. Evocation of inspiration. Magic art. Get ready to write immediately. I reason too much.

Immediate work, even poor, is better than dreaming.

A succession of small wills produces a great result.

[Immediate work, even bad, is better than dreaming.]

Every recoil of the will is a particle of lost substance. How hesitation is therefore prodigal! And one may judge this by the immensity of the final effort necessary to repair so many losses!

The man who prays in the evening is a captain who positions his sentinels. He can sleep.

Dreams of Death & Warnings.

I have so far enjoyed my memories alone; they must be enjoyed by two. Make the raptures of the heart a passion.

Because I perceive a glorious existence, I believe I am capable of realizing it. O Jean-Jacques!

Work forcibly engenders good mores, sobriety, and chastity, consequently health, wealth, successive and progressive genius, and charity. *Age quod agis*.

Fish, cold baths, showers, lichen, pastilles occasionally; moreover, the suppression of all stimulants.

Lichen from Iceland .... 125 gr.
White Sugar .... 250 gr.

Soak the lichen, for 12 to 15 hours, in a sufficient quantity of cold water, then discard the water.

Boil the lichen in 2 liters of water over a gentle and sustained flame, until the two liters are reduced to one, remove the froth once; add the 250 grams of sugar and allow to thicken until the consistency of syrup.

Let cool. Take *three* very large spoonfuls per day (in the morning, at noon, and in the evening). Do not be afraid to increase doses, if the crises are too frequent.

93

HYGIENE · CONDUCT · METHOD

I swear to myself to henceforth adopt the following rules as the eternal rules of my life:

Pray every morning to God, a reservoir of all strength and of all [good] justice, to my father, to Mariette, and to Poe, as intercessors; to ask them to grant me *the necessary strength* to accomplish all my duties, and to grant my mother *a long enough life* to enjoy my transformation; work all day, or at least as long *as my strength permits*; to trust myself to God, that is, to Justice itself, for the success of my projects; make a new prayer every evening, to ask God for life & strength for my mother & for myself; four parts, — one for my daily life, one for my creditors, one for my friends, and one for my mother; — obey the principles of the strictest sobriety, the first of which is the suppression of all stimulants, whatever they may be.

93 A

HYGIENE · MORALITY · CONDUCT

Too late, perhaps! — My mother and Jeanne. — My health out of charity, out of duty! — Diseases of Jeanne. Infirmities, loneliness of my mother.

— Do your duty every day & trust God, for the next day.

— The only way to earn money is to work in a disinterested manner.

— An abridged wisdom. Grooming, prayer, work.

— Prayer: charity, wisdom, strength.

— Without charity, I am only but a tintinnabulating cymbal.

— My humiliations have been but blessings from God.

— Is my phase of egoism finished?

— The faculty of responding to the necessity of each minute, exactitude, in a word, must infallibly find its reward.

"The misfortune which is perpetuated produces on the soul the effect of old age upon the body; one can no longer move; one goes to bed...

On the other hand, one derives from extreme youth reasons for procrastination; when one has plenty of time to squander, one is persuaded that one can wait years before gambling on events."

CHATEAUBRIAND

93 B
HYGIENE · CONDUCT · METHOD

(Extracts from Emerson's *The Conduct of Life*)

Great men... have not been boasters and buffoons, but perceivers of *the terror of life*, and have manned themselves to face it.

"Fate is nothing but the deeds committed in a prior state of existence."

"What we wish for in youth, comes in heaps on us in old age," too often cursed with the granting of our prayer: and hence the high caution, that since we are sure of having what we wish we beware to ask only for high things.

The one prudence in life is concentration; the one evil is dissipation.

The poet Campbell said that "a man accustomed to work was equal to any achievement he resolved on, and that, for himself necessity, not inspiration, was the prompter of his muse."

In our daily affairs a decision must be made, — the best, if you can; but any is better than none.

The second substitute for temperament is drill, the power of use and routine.

"More are made good by exercitation than by nature," said Democritus.

Mirabeau said: "Why should we feel ourselves to be men, unless it be to succeed in everything, everywhere. You must say of nothing: *That is beneath me*, nor feel that anything can be out of your power. Nothing is impossible to the man who can will. *Is that necessary? That shall be.* This is the only *Law of success.*"

We acquire the strength we have overcome.

The hero is he who is immovably centred.

The main difference between people seems to be, that one man can come under obligations on which you can rely;

and another is not. *As he has not a law within him, there's nothing to tie him to.*

If you would be powerful, pretend to be powerful.
Seeketh though great things? seek them not.

Conduct of Life

— Great men have not been [...] for high things.

— His heart (was) the throne of will.

— Life is search after power.

— No honest seeking goes unrewarded.

— We must reckon success a constitutional trait.

— The one prudence [...] of his muse.

— A decision [...] said Democritus.

— *Pecunia alter sanguis.*

— Mirabeau said [...] immovably centred.

— Your theories and plans of life are fair and commendable; — but will you stick?

— If you [...] powerful.

MY HEART LAID BARE

MY HEARTLAND BABE

1

Of the vaporization and centralization of the *Ego*. Everything is there.

Of a certain sensual rapture in the company of debauchees.

(I intend to begin *My Heart Laid Bare* no matter where, no matter how, and continue it from day to day, following the inspiration of the day *&* the circumstance, provided the inspiration is spirited.)

2

The first arrival, provided that he knows how to amuse, has the right to speak of himself.

3

I understand how one can abandon a cause so as to discover what can be experienced when serving another.

It would perhaps be sweet to be alternately victim and executioner.

4

Stupidities of Girardin
"We are accustomed to taking the bull *by the horns.* Let us then take the speech by *the conclusion.*" (November 7, 1863)
Thus, Girardin believes that the horns of bulls are planted on their asses. He confuses the horns with the tail.

That before imitating the Ptolemies of French journalism, the Belgian journalists take the trouble to reflect on the question which I have been studying for thirty years in all its aspects, as will be proved by the volume that will shortly appear under this title: QUESTIONS DE PRESSE; that they do not hasten to treat with *sovereign ridicule** an opinion which is as true as it is true that the earth revolves *&* that the sun does not revolve.

ÉMILE DE GIRARDIN

* *"There are people who pretend that nothing prevents them from believing that, the sky being motionless, it is the earth which revolves around its axis. But these people do not realize, because of what is happening around us, how their opinion is* sovereignly ridiculous (πανυ γελοιότατον)."

PTOLEMY, *The Almagest*, Bk. I, Ch. VI

Et habet mea mentrita meatum.

GIRARDIN.

5

For

MY HEART LAID BARE

Woman is the opposite of the Dandy.

Therefore she must inspire horror.

Woman is hungry and she wants to eat. Thirsty, and she wants to drink.

She is rutting and she wants to be fucked.

Beautiful merit!

Woman is *natural*, that is, abominable.

Thus, she is always vulgar, that is, the opposite of the Dandy.

———

Concerning the Legion of Honor.

He who seeks the cross seems to say: If you do not decorate me for doing my duty, I will not do it again.

— If a man has merit, what is the use of decorating him? If he has none, he can be decorated, for it will give him luster.

To consent to be decorated is to acknowledge that the State or a prince has the right to judge you, to dignify you, etc.

———

Besides, if not pride, Christian humility forbids this cross.

Calculation in favor of God.
Nothing exists without a purpose.
Therefore my existence has a purpose. What purpose? I don't know.
It was not therefore I who marked it.
It is therefore a more learned man than myself.
I must therefore ask someone to enlighten me. This is the wisest course of action.

The Dandy must aspire to be sublime without interruption; he must live & sleep before a mirror.

6

Analysis of counter-religions: example of sacred prostitution.

What is sacred prostitution?

Nervous excitation.

Mysticalness of paganism.

Mysticism — a link between Paganism *&* Christianism.

Paganism *&* Christianism — reciprocal proofs.

The Revolution and the Cult of Reason prove the idea of sacrifice.

Superstition is the reservoir of all truths.

7

There is in all change something both infamous and enjoyable, something that is due to infidelity and moving house. This suffices to explain the French Revolution.

8

My intoxication in 1848.
What was the nature of that intoxication?
A taste for revenge. The *natural* pleasure of demolition.
[My fury at the coup d'État.]
[How many times I was shot at.]
Literary intoxication; memory of readings.
May 15th. — Always the taste for destruction. Legitimate taste, if everything that is natural is legitimate.
[My fury at the coup d'État.]

The horrors of June. The madness of the people and the madness of the bourgeoisie. Natural love of crime.

My fury at the coup d'État. How many times I was shot at! Another Bonaparte! what shame!

And yet everyone is pacified. Has the President no law to invoke?

What Emperor Napoléon III is. What he is worth. Find the explanation of his nature, & his providentiality.

9

To be a useful man always seemed to me something quite hideous.

―――――

1848 was amusing only because everybody made utopias like castles in Spain.

1848 was charming only because of the very excess of the Ridiculous.

―――――

Robespierre is estimable only because he has made some beautiful phrases.

10

The Revolution, through sacrifice, confirms superstition.

11

POLITICS

I have no convictions, as the people of my century understand, because I have no ambition.

There is no foundation in myself for a conviction.

There is a certain cowardice, or rather, a certain feebleness, as among honest people.

The brigands alone are convinced, — of what? — that they must succeed. Therefore, they succeed.

Why should I succeed, since I don't even want to try?

One can found glorious empires on crime, and noble religions on imposture.

Nevertheless, I have some convictions, in a higher sense, and which can not be understood by the people of my time.

12

Feeling of *solitude*, since my childhood. Despite the family, — and among my comrades, above all, — feeling of an eternally solitary destiny.

However, a very keen taste for life & for pleasure.

13

Almost our whole life is used for foolish curiosities. Contrarily, there are things which should excite the curiosity of men to the highest degree, and which, judging from their customary ways of life, do not inspire any of them.

Where are our dead friends?
Why are we here?
Do we come from somewhere?
What is freedom?
Can it agree with providential law?
Is the number of souls finite or infinite?
And the number of habitable lands?
Etc., etc.

14

Nations have great men only despite themselves. Hence, the great man is the conqueror of his entire nation.

The ridiculous modern Religions:
Molière,
Béranger,
Garibaldi.

15

Belief in progress is a doctrine of the slothful, a doctrine of the *Belgians*. It is the individual who relies on his neighbors to do his work.

There can be no (true, that is, moral) progress but in the individual and by the individual alone.

But the world is made up of people who can think only in common, in herds. Thus the *Belgian Societies*.

There are also people who can amuse themselves only in hordes. The true hero amuses himself alone.

16

Eternal superiority of the Dandy.
What is the Dandy?

17

My opinions on the theater. What I have always found most beautiful in a theater, in my childhood, and still now, is *the chandelier* — a beautiful, luminous object: crystalline, complicated, circular, and symmetrical.

However, I do not absolutely deny the value of dramatic literature. Only, I would like the actors to be mounted on very high pattens, wearing masks more expressive than the human face, and to recite through speaking-trumpets; finally, that the roles of women be played by men.

After all, whether seen through the large or the small end of a lorgnette, the chandelier always seemed to me the principal actor.

18

One must work, if not out of taste, at least out of despair, since, as is well verified, to work is less boring than to amuse oneself.

19

There is in every man, at every moment, two simultaneous postulations: one toward God, the other toward Satan. Invocation of God, or spirituality, is a desire to rise in rank; that of Satan, or animality, is the joy to descend. It is to the latter that love for women and intimate conversations with animals, dogs, cats, etc. must be related.

The joys that are derived from those two loves are adapted to the nature of those two loves.

20

Intoxication of Humanity.
Great picture to be made:
    in the sense of charity;
    in the sense of libertinage;
    in the literary or dramaturgic sense.

21

The question (torture) is, like the art of discovering truth, a barbarous silliness; it is the application of a material means to a Spiritual end.

———

The Death Penalty is the result of a mystical idea, entirely misunderstood today. The Death Penalty is not intended to *save* Society, materially at least. Its purpose is to *save* (Spiritually) Society and the guilty. For the Sacrifice to be perfect, there must be assent *&* joy on the part of the victim. Giving chloroform to a condemned man would be an impiety, for it would be to take away the Consciousness of his grandeur as a victim and eliminate his chances of gaining Paradise.

———

As for torture, it is born of the infamous aspect of man's heart: thirsting for rapture. Cruelty and rapture, identical Sensations, like extreme heat and extreme cold.

22

What I think of the vote and the right of election. Of the rights of man.

That which is vile in any function.

A Dandy does nothing.

Can you imagine a Dandy speaking to the people, except to scorn them?

There is no reasonable and assured government but the aristocratic.

Monarchies or republics based on democracy are equally absurd and weak.

Great nausea of advertisements.

There exist but three respectable beings:

The priest, the warrior, the poet. To know, to kill, & to create.

The other men are tallieable and corvéable, made for the stable, that is, for exercising what one calls *professions*.

23

Let us observe that the abolishers of the death penalty must be more or less *interested* in abolishing it.

Often, they are guillotinists. This can be summarized as follows: "I want to be able to cut off your head, but you shall not touch mine."

The abolishers of the soul (*materialists*) are [naturally] ‹necessarily› the abolishers of *hell*; they are, it's a sure blow, *interested*.

At the least, they are people who are *afraid of rebirth*, — the slothful.

24

Madame de Metternich, although a princess, has forgotten to answer me in regard to what I have said of her and Wagner.

Mores of the 19th century.

25

The story of my translation of *Edgar Poe*.
The story of *Les fleurs du Mal*. Humiliation by misunderstanding, and my trial.

History of my relations with all the famous men of that time.

Pretty portraits of some imbeciles:
    Clément de Ris.
    Castagnary.
Portraits of magistrates, officials, newspaper editors, etc.
Portrait of the artist, in general.

The editor-in-chief and the pawn. Great taste of all French people for being pawned, & for dictatorship. It's the: "If I were king!"

Portraits & anecdotes.
François, — Buloz, — Houssaye, — the famous Rouy, — de Calonne, — Charpentier, — who corrects his authors, by virtue of the equality given to all men by the immortal principles of 89; — Chevalier, a true editor-in-chief according to the Empire.

26

On *George Sand*

The woman Sand is the Prudhomme of immorality. She has always been a moralist.

Only she used to be counter-morality. — Also she was never an artist.

She has that celebrated *flowing style*, dear to the bourgeois.

She is stupid, she is heavy, she is talkative; she has, in [morality] moral ideas, the same depth of judgment and the same delicacy of feeling as concierges *&* financed daughters.

What she says about her mother.

What she says about poetry.

Her love [of] for the working class.

That some men may have been enamored of this latrine is proof of the abasement of the men of this age.

See the preface to *Mademoiselle La Quintinie*, where she claims that true Christians do not believe in Hell. Sand is for the *God of good people*, the god of concierges *&* thieving servants. She has good reasons for wanting to eliminate Hell.

27

THE DEVIL AND GEORGE SAND

It must not be believed that the Devil only tempts men of genius. He doubtless despises imbeciles, but he does not disdain their competition. Quite the contrary, he founds his great hopes on them.

Take George Sand. She is, above all, and more than anything else, a *big beast*; but she is *possessed*. It was the Devil who persuaded her to trust *her good heart* and *her common sense*, therewith she might persuade all other big beasts to trust their good hearts and their common sense.

I cannot think of this stupid creature without a certain shudder of horror. If I met her, I could not help but throw a stoup at her head.

28

George Sand is one of those old ingénues who never want to leave the boards.

I have lately read a preface (the preface to *Mademoiselle La Quintinie*) where she claims that a true Christian can not believe in Hell.

[There are] She has good reasons for wanting to eliminate Hell.

[28 A]

The Religion of the woman Sand. Preface to *Mademoiselle La Quintinie*. The woman Sand is interested in believing that Hell does not exist.

29

I am bored in France, especially because everyone resembles Voltaire.

Emerson forgot Voltaire in his *Representative Men*. He could have made a pretty chapter entitled: *Voltaire*, or *The Anti-Poet*, the king of the strollers, the prince of superficials, the anti-artist, the preacher of concierges, [the Mother Gig] the Father Gigogne of the editors of *Siècle*.

30

In *The Ears of the Earl of Chesterfield*, Voltaire jokes about this immortal soul that had resided for nine months between excrement & urine. Voltaire, like all the slothful, hates mystery.*

Not being able to eliminate love, the Church at least wanted to disinfect it, and so she made marriage.

* At least he could have guessed in this environment the malice or satire of providence against love, and, in the act of generation, a sign of original sin. In fact, we can only make love with excretory organs.

31

Portrait of the Literary Rabble.

Doctor Estaminétus Crapulosus Pédantissimus. His portrait made in the manner of Praxiteles.

His pipe.
His opinions.
His Hegelianism.
His filth.
His ideas on art.
His bile.
His jealousy.
A pretty picture of modern youth.

32

Φαρμακοτριβης ανερ και τῶν τους οφεις ες τα θαυματα τρεφοντων.[5]

ÉLIEN (?)

---

5. Citation from Claudius Élien's (175–235 CE) *Περὶ Ζῴων Ἰδιότητος* [*De Natura Animalum*], IX, 62. "The concocter of medicine is among those who feed serpents to obtain prodigies."

33

Theology.
What is the fall?
If it is unity become duality, it is God who has fallen.
In other words, would not creation be the fall of God?

Dandyism.
What is the superior man?
He is not the specialist.
He is the man of Leisure and of Broad Education.
To be rich and to love work.

34

Why does the man of spirit love girls more than worldly women, even though they are equally stupid?
— To figure out.

35

There are certain women who resemble the ribbon of the Legion of Honor. They are no longer desired because they have been soiled by certain men.

It is for the same reason that I would not put on the pants of a lepidote.

What is annoying in love is that it is a crime in which one cannot do without [some] an accomplice.

36

Study of the Great Illness of the horror of Home. Reasons for the Disease. Progressive growth of the Disease.

Indignation caused by the universal fatuity of all classes, of all beings, in both sexes, in all ages.

Man loves man so much that, when he flees the city, it is still to seek the crowd, that is, to remake the city in the country.

37

Speech of Durandeau on the Japanese. (Me! I am French before all.) The Japanese are monkeys. It is Darjon who told me that.

Speech by the physician, the friend of Mathieu, on the art of not making children, on Moses, & on the immortality of the soul.

Art is a civilizing agent (Castagnary).

38

Physiognomy of a sage and of his family, on the sixth floor, drinking café au lait.

Sir Nacquart the father *&* Sir Nacquart the son.
How the Nacquart son became advisor to the Court of Appeal.

39

Of love, of the predilection of the French for military metaphors. Every metaphor here bears a mustache.

Militant literature.
Manning the breach.
Carrying the flag high.
Holding the flag high and firm.
Throwing yourself into the fray.
One of the veterans.

All these glorious phrases are generally applied to the prigs and the lazybones of the tavern.

40

French Metaphors

Soldier of the judicial press (Bertin).
The militant press.

41

To be added to military metaphors:
Poets of combat.
Avant-garde litterateurs.
The use of military metaphors denotes non-militant spirits, but ones made for discipline, that is, for conformity, spirits born domestic, Belgian spirits, who can think only in crowds.

42

The taste for pleasure binds us to the present. The care for our salvation suspends us for the future.

[The man] He who attaches himself to pleasure, that is, to the present, makes me think of the effect of a man rolling on a slope and who, in trying to cling to the shrubs, uproots and carries them away in his fall.

Above all, TO BE *a great man* and *a Saint* for oneself.

43

Of the hatred of the people contra beauty.
Examples.
Jeanne *&* Madame Muller.

44

POLITICS

In sum, in view of history and in view of the people of France, the great glory of Napoléon III [had been] will have been to prove that the first to arrive can, by seizing the telegraph and the National Printing Office, govern a great nation.

Those who believe that such things can be accomplished without the permission of the people are imbeciles, — and those who believe that glory can only be supported by virtue are imbeciles!

Dictators are the servants of the people, — nothing more, — a foolish part elsewhere, — and glory is [the result] [the accom.] the result of the adaptation of a spirit with national stupidity.

45

What is love?
The need for self-abandonment.
Man is a worshipping animal.
To worship is to sacrifice and prostitute oneself.
Therefore all love is prostitution.

[45 A]

The most prostituted being is the being *par excellence*, it is God, since he is the supreme friend of every individual, since he is the common, inexhaustible reservoir of love.

[45 B]
PRAYER

Do not chastise me in my mother, nor chasten my mother because of me. — I commend the souls of my father and of Mariette. — Give me the strength to immediately do my duty every day and to consequently become a hero and a Saint.

46

A chapter on indestructible, eternal, universal, and ingenious human ferocity.

Of the love of blood.

Of the intoxication of blood.

Of the intoxication of crowds.

Of the intoxication of the tortured (Damiens).

47

The poet, the priest, and the soldier are the only great men among men:

the man who sings, the man who blesses, and the man who sacrifices and who sacrifices himself.

The rest are made for the whip.

Let us defy the people, common sense, the heart, inspiration, and evidence.

48

I have always been astonished that one lets women enter churches. What conversation can they have with God?

The eternal Venus (caprice, hysteria, fantasy) is one of the seductive forms of the Devil.

The day when the young writer corrects his first proof, he is as proud as a schoolboy who has just caught his first pox.

Do not forget a great chapter on the art of divination, by water, maps, examination of the hand, etc.

49

Woman does not know how to distinguish the soul from the body. She is simplistic, like animals. — A satirist would say that it is because she has nothing but a body.

———

A chapter on:
  Grooming
The Morality of Grooming.
The Happiness of Grooming.

50

From the priggery
    of professors
    of judges
    of priests,
and of ministers.

The pretty great men of the day.
    Renan.
    Feydeau.
    Octave Feuillet.
    Scholl.

The editors of newspapers: François Buloz, Houssaye, Rouy, Girardin, Texier, de Calonne, Solar, Turgan, Dalloz.
— List of scoundrels. Solar at the head.

51

Being a great man and a saint *for oneself*, there is the only important thing.

52

Nadar, he is the most astonishing expression of vitality. Adrien told me that his brother Félix had all the viscera in duplicate. I have been jealous of him, to see him so successful in everything that is not abstract.

Veuillot is so crude and such an enemy of the arts that one would say that the whole *Democracy* of the world had taken refuge in his breast.

Development of the portrait.

Supremacy of the pure idea, in the Christian as in the Babouvian communist.

Fanaticism of humility. Do not even aspire to understand Religion.

53

Music.
Of slavery.
Of the women of the world.
Of prostitutes.
Of magistrates.
Of sacraments.
The man of letters is the enemy of the world.
Of bureaucrats.

54

In [politics] love, as in nearly all human affairs, the entente cordiale is the result of a misunderstanding. This misunderstanding, it is the pleasure. The man cries: "O my angel!" The woman coos: "Mama! mama!" And those two fools are persuaded that they think in unison. — The inviolable abyss, which creates incommunicability, remains inviolate.

55

Why is the spectacle of the sea so infinitely & so eternally pleasing?

Because the sea evokes both the idea of immensity and of movement. Six or seven leagues represent for man the radius of the infinite. There's a diminutive infinity. Of what importance if it suffices to suggest the idea of the total infinite? Twelve or fourteen leagues (on the diameter), twelve or fourteen of liquid in motion suffice to give the highest idea of beauty that is offered to man in his transitory dwelling.

56

There is nothing interesting on earth but its religions.

What is the Universal Religion? (Chateaubriand, de Maistre, the Alexandrians, Capé.)

There is a Universal Religion, made for the Alchemists of Thought, a Religion that frees itself of man, considered as a divine memento.

57

Saint-Marc Girardin said a phrase that will remain: *Let us be mediocre*.

Let us set that phrase beside this one of Robespierre: "Those who do not believe in the immortality of their being do themselves justice."

The phrase of Saint-Marc Girardin implies a great hatred for the sublime.

Whoever sees Saint-Marc Girardin walking down the street immediately conceives of the idea of a large goose infatuated with itself, but frightened and running on the high road, before conscientiousness.

58

Theory of true civilization.

It rests not in gas, nor in steam, nor in table-turning. It rests in the diminution of the traces of original sin.

Nomads, shepherds, hunters, agriculturists, and even cannibals, *all* may be superior, in energy, in personal dignity, to our races of the West.

We perhaps shall be destroyed.

Theocracy *&* Communism.

59

It is through [idleness] leisure that I have, in part, grown, to my great detriment; for leisure, without wealth, increases debts, the insults resulting from debts.

But, to my great advantage, with respect to sensitivity, to meditation, and to the faculty of dandyism & of dilettantism.

The other men of letters are, for the most part, very ignorant vile gleaners.

60

The young girl of editors.
The young girl of editors-in-chief.
The young girl as scarecrow, monster, murderer of art.
The young girl, what she is in reality.

A little fool and a little slut; the greatest imbecile united with the greatest depravity.

There is in the young girl all the abjection of the rogue and the schoolboy.

61

Advice to non-communists:
Everything is common, even God.

62

The Frenchman is such a well-domesticated barnyard animal that he dares not climb over any fences. See his tastes in art & in literature.

He is an animal of the Latin race; filth in his home does not displease him, and in literature, he is scatophagous. He is crazy for excrement. Litterateurs call this the *Gallic soil*.

A fine example of French baseness, of the nation that claims to be independent before all others.

> *The following extract from M. de Vaulabelle's fine book will suffice to give an idea of the impression made by the escape of Lavalette on the less enlightened portion of the Royalist party:*

> "At this moment of the Second Restoration, the Royalist agitation went as far as madness. The young Josephine de Lavalette was educated in one of the principal convents of Paris (the Abbaye-au-Bois); she had left it only to come and embrace her father. When she returned after the escape, and the very modest part she had taken there was known, a great clamor was raised against this child; the nuns and her companions fled from her, and many parents declared that they would withdraw their

daughters if she was kept. They did not wish, they said, to leave their children in contact with a young person who had engaged in such conduct and given such an example. When Madame de Lavalette recovered her liberty, six weeks later, she was obliged to take back her daughter."

63

Princes and Generations

There is an equal injustice in attributing to reigning princes the merits and vices of the present people whom they govern.

These merits and vices are almost always, as statistics and logic can demonstrate, attributable to the atmosphere of the previous government.

Louis XIV inherits the men of Louis XIII. Glory.
Napoléon I inherits the men of the Republic. Glory.
Louis-Philippe inherits the men of Charles X. Glory.
Napoléon III inherits the men of Louis-Philippe. Dishonor.

It is always the preceding government that is responsible for the mores of its successor, in so far as a government can be responsible for anything.

The abrupt breaks that circumstances bring to a reign do not allow this law to be absolutely exact, relative to time. One cannot mark exactly where influence ends — but this influence will subsist throughout the generation that underwent it in its youth.

64

Of the hatred of youth against quoters. The quoter is for them an enemy.

I would put orthography itself under the hand of the executioner. (Th. Gautier)

Beautiful painting to be made: The Literary Rabble.

Do not forget a portrait of Forgues, the Pirate, the Skimmer of Letters.

The invincible taste for prostitution in the heart of man, from whence is born its horror of solitude. — He wants to be *two*. The man of genius wants to be *one*, thus solitary.
Glory is to remain *one*, and to prostitute oneself in a particular manner.
It is this horror of solitude, this need to lose one's *ego* in the external flesh, which man nobly calls *the need to love*.

Two fine Religions, immortalized upon Walls, eternal obsessions of the People: a cock (the ancient phallus) — & "Vive Barbès!" or "Down with Philippe" or "Vive la République!"

65

To study, in all its modes, in the works of nature and in the works of man, the eternal and universal law of gradation, *bit by bit, little by little*, with progressively increasing forces, as well as compound interests, in terms of finance.

It is the same with *artistic and literary skill*; it is the same with the variable treasure of the *will*.

66

The crowd of little litterateurs, who we see at funerals, distributing handshakes, and commending themselves to the memory of the rapporteurs of gossip columns.

From the burials of famous men.

67

Molière. My opinion of *Tartuffe* is that it is not a comedy, but a pamphlet. With regard to this play, an atheist, if he is simply a well-bred man, will think that one should never give certain serious questions to the rabble.

68

To glorify the cult of images (my great, my sole, my primitive passion).

To glorify vagabondage and what one could call Bohemianism, the cult of multiplied sensation, expressing itself through music. Refer here to Liszt.

———

Of the need of beating women.
One can chastise what one loves. Herewith children. But this implies the pain of despising that which one loves.

———

Of cuckolding and of cuckolds.
The sorrow of the cuckold.
It arises from his pride, from a false reasoning about honor & happiness, and from a love foolishly diverted from God to be attributed to creatures.
It is always the worshipping animal deceiving itself about its idol.

69

Analysis of insolent imbecility. Clément de Ris *&* Paul Pérignon.

70

The more man cultivates the arts, the less he gets hard.
There is a growing divorce of feeling between the spirit and the brute.
The brute alone is hard, and fucking is the lyricism of the people.

To fuck is to aspire to enter someone else, and the artist never leaves himself.

I forgot the name of that slut … ah! bah! I shall remember it at the last judgment.

Music conveys the idea of space.
All the arts, more or less; since they are *number* and number is a translation of space.

Want every day to be the greatest of men!!!

71

As a child, I sometimes wanted to be pope, but a military pope, sometimes an actor.

What raptures I derived from those two hallucinations.

72

As a child, I felt in my heart two contradictory feelings: the horror of life & the ecstasy of life.

It is indeed the reality of a nervous sloth.

73

Nations have great men only in spite of themselves.

———

About the actor and my childhood dreams, a chapter on that which constitutes, in the human soul, the actor's vocation, the glory of the actor, the art of the actor, and his situation in the world.

The theory of Legouvé. Is Legouvé a cold jester, a Swift, who tried to see if France [would] could swallow a new absurdity?

His choice. Good in the sense that Samson is not an actor. Of the true greatness of pariahs.

———

Perhaps even virtue is injurious to the talents of pariahs.

74

Commerce is, in its essence, *satanic*.

— Commerce is the lender made; it is a loan with the implication: *Give me more than I give you.*

— The spirit of every merchant is completely depraved.

— Commerce is *natural, therefore it is villainous*.

— The least vile of all businessmen is the one who says: "Let us be virtuous so as to earn much more money than the fools who are deceitful."

— For the businessman, honesty itself is a speculation about lucre.

— Commerce is satanic, because it is one of the forms of egoism, & the lowest, & the most vile.

75

When Jesus Christ said:
"Blessed are those who are hungry, for they shall be satisfied!" he was gambling on probabilities.

76

The world functions only through Misunderstanding.

— It is by Universal Misunderstanding that all the world agrees.

— For if, by misfortune, we understood one another, we would never agree.

The man of wit, who will never agree with anyone, must dedicate himself to loving the conversation of imbeciles and the reading of bad books. He will derive bitter raptures that will more than compensate for his fatigue.

77

A certain functionary, a minister, a director of a theater or of a newspaper, can sometimes be estimable beings; but they can never be divine. They are people without personality, unoriginal beings, born for a function, that is, for public service.

78

God & his depth.

One can not lack spirit and seek in God the accomplice and the friend who are always lacking. God is the eternal confidant in this tragedy of which everyone is the hero. There may be usurers and assassins who say to God: "Lord, make my next enterprise succeed!" But the prayers of these villainous people do not spoil the honor and pleasure of my own.

79

Every idea is, in itself, endowed with immortal life, like a person.

Every created form, even by man, is immortal. Because form is independent of matter, & it is not molecules that constitute form.

Anecdotes pertaining to Émile Douay & to Constantin Guys, destroying, or rather believing to destroy their works.

80

It is impossible [to open] to glance through any newspaper, no matter what day, or what month, or what year, without finding in every line the signs of the most appalling human perversity, together with the most surprising *boasts* about probity, about kindness, about charity, and the boldest affirmations regarding progress and civilization.

Every newspaper, from the first to the last line, is only a tissue of horrors. Wars, crimes, thefts, impudicities, tortures, crimes of princes, crimes of nations, crimes of individuals, an intoxication of universal atrocity.

And it is with this disgusting aperitif that civilized man accompanies his every morning meal. Everything, in this world, transudes crime: the newspaper, the wall, *&* the face of man.

I do not understand how a pure hand can touch a newspaper without a convulsion of disgust.

81

The strength of the amulet demonstrated by philosophy. The pierced coins, the talismans, each person's memories.

Treaty about Moral Dynamics.
Of the Virtue of Sacraments.

From my childhood, a tendency to mysticalness. My conversations with God.

82

Of Obsession, of Possession, of Prayer *&* of Faith.
Moral Dynamic of Jesus.
(Renan finds it ridiculous that Jesus believes in the omnipotence, even material, of Prayer *&* of Faith.)

The sacraments are the means of this Dynamic.

Of the infamy of printing, a great obstacle to the development of the Beautiful.

Beautiful conspiracy to organize for the extermination of the Jewish Race.
The Jews, *Librarians* and witnesses of *Redemption*.

83

All the imbeciles of the Bourgeoisie who incessantly utter the words: "immoral, immorality, morality in art" and other nonsense, remind me of Louise Villedieu, a five-franc whore, who accompanied me one time to the Louvre, where she had never gone, began to blush, to cover her face, and tugging me every moment by the sleeve, asked me before the statues and the immortal paintings, how one could publicly display such indecencies.

The vine leaves of Sir Nieuwerkerke.

84

For the law of progress to exist, everyone [must] would have to create it; that is, when every individual will apply himself to progress, then, & only then, will humanity be in a state of progress.

This hypothesis can serve to explain the identity of two contradictory ideas: liberty & fatality. — Not only will there be, in the case of progress, an identity between freedom & fatality, but this identity has always existed. This identity is *history*, the history of nations and of individuals.

85

Sonnet to be quoted in My Heart Laid Bare.
Also quote the play on Roland.

I dreamt that night when Philis returned,
Beautiful as she was in the light of day,
That she wanted her ghost to again make love,
And that, like Ixion, I embrace a cloud.

Her shadow slips totally naked into my bed,
And says to me: "Dear Damon, here I return;
I only made this sad visit
Where, since my departure, Fate has restrained me.

"I come to kiss again the most beautiful of lovers;
I come to die again in thine embraces!"
Then, when this idol had abused my flame,

She said to me: "Adieu! I must return to the dead.
As you boasted of having fucked my body,
You can boast of having fucked my soul."

Satyrique Parnassus.

I believe that this sonnet is by Maynard.
Malassis pretends that it is by Racan.

**HYGIENE. CONDUCT.
METHOD. MORALITY.**

PRECIOUS NOTES

[THOUGHTS &
APHORISMS]

HYGIENE · CONDUCT · METHOD · MORALITY

86

FLARES · HYGIENE · PROJECTS

"The more one wills, the better one wills."

The more one [wills] works, the better one works, and the more one wants to work. The more one produces, the more fertile one becomes.

After a debauchery, one always feels more alone, more abandoned.

Morally as physically, I have always had the sensation of the abyss, not only of the abyss of sleep, but the abyss of action, of dream, of memory, of desire, of regret, of remorse, of beauty, of number, etc.

I have cultivated my hysteria with rapture and terror. [Today] Now, I always have vertigo, and today, January 23, 1862, I have suffered a singular warning: I have felt the *wind of the wing of imbecility* pass over me.

87

HYGIENE · MORALITY

To Honfleur! as soon as possible, before falling further down.

How many presentiments and signs already sent by God, that it is *high time* to act, to regard the present minute as the most important of minutes, and to make a *perpetual rapture* of my ordinary torment, that is, of Work!

88

HYGIENE · CONDUCT · MORALITY

At every minute we are crushed by the idea and the sensation of time. And there are only two means of escaping this nightmare, — to forget it: Pleasure and Work. Pleasure consumes us. Work fortifies us. Let us choose.

The more we use one of these means, the more [we flee] the other inspires us with repugnance.

One can forget time only by using it.

[De Maistre & Edgar]

Everything is done little by little.

FLARES

De Maistre & Edgar Poe taught me to reason.

There is no long work but that which one dares not begin. It becomes a nightmare.

89

HYGIENE

By postponing what one has to do, one runs the risk of never being able to do it. By postponing conversion, one risks being damned.

To cure everything, misery, sickness, and melancholy, there is absolutely nothing but the *Taste of Work*.

90

PRECIOUS NOTES

Do every day what duty and prudence want.
If you work every day, life will be more bearable.
Work *six* days without relent.

To find subjects, γνῶθι σεαυτόν ... (List of my tastes.)

Always be a poet, even in prose. Grand style (nothing is more beautiful than the commonplace).

First begin, and then make use of logic & analysis. Every hypothesis wants its conclusion.

Find the daily frenzy.

91

HYGIENE · CONDUCT · MORALITY

TWO PARTS:

Debts (Ancelle).
Friends (*my mother, friends, myself*).
Thus, 1,000 francs must be divided into two parts of 500 francs each, and the second divided into *three* parts.

To Honfleur

Make a review and ranking of all my *letters* (2 days).
And all my debts (2 days). (Four categories: *banknotes, big debts, small debts, friends.*)
Classification of engravings (2 days).
Ranking of notes (2 days).

92

HYGIENE · CONDUCT · METHOD

Jeanne 300, my mother 200, myself 300. 800 francs per month. To work from six in the morning, till noon, on an empty stomach. Working blindly, aimlessly, like a madman. We shall see the result.

I suppose I base my destiny on several hours of uninterrupted work.

Everything is reparable. There is still time. Who knows even if new pleasures...?

Glory, payment of my Debts. *Wealth* of Jeanne and of my mother.

I have not yet known the pleasure of a fulfilled plan. The power of a dominant idea. The power of Hope.

The habit of accomplishing one's Duty dispels fear. One must want to dream and know how to dream. Evocation of inspiration. Magic art. Get ready to write immediately. I reason too much.

Immediate work, even poor, is better than dreaming.

A succession of small wills produces a great result.

[Immediate work, even bad, is better than dreaming.]

Every recoil of the will is a particle of lost substance. How hesitation is therefore prodigal! And one may judge this by the immensity of the final effort necessary to repair so many losses!

The man who prays in the evening is a captain who positions his sentinels. He can sleep.

Dreams of Death *&* Warnings.

I have so far enjoyed my memories alone; they must be enjoyed by two. Make the raptures of the heart a passion.

Because I perceive a glorious existence, I believe I am capable of realizing it. O Jean-Jacques!

Work forcibly engenders good mores, sobriety, and chastity, consequently health, wealth, successive and progressive genius, and charity. *Age quod agis*.

Fish, cold baths, showers, lichen, pastilles occasionally; moreover, the suppression of all stimulants.

Lichen from Iceland	125 gr.
White Sugar	250 gr.

Soak the lichen, for 12 to 15 hours, in a sufficient quantity of cold water, then discard the water.

Boil the lichen in 2 liters of water over a gentle and sustained flame, until the two liters are reduced to one, remove the froth once; add the 250 grams of sugar and allow to thicken until the consistency of syrup.

Let cool. Take *three* very large spoonfuls per day (in the morning, at noon, and in the evening). Do not be afraid to increase doses, if the crises are too frequent.

93

HYGIENE · CONDUCT · METHOD

I swear to myself to henceforth adopt the following rules as the eternal rules of my life:

Pray every morning to God, a reservoir of all strength and of all [good] *justice, to my father, to Mariette, and to Poe,* as intercessors; to ask them to grant me *the necessary strength* to accomplish all my duties, and to grant my mother *a long enough life* to enjoy my transformation; work all day, or at least as long *as my strength permits*; to trust myself to God, that is, to Justice itself, for the success of my projects; make a new prayer every evening, to ask God for life & strength for my mother & for myself; four parts, — one for my daily life, one for my creditors, one for my friends, and one for my mother; — obey the principles of the strictest sobriety, the first of which is the suppression of all stimulants, whatever they may be.

93 A

HYGIENE · MORALITY · CONDUCT

Too late, perhaps! — My mother and Jeanne. — My health out of charity, out of duty! — Diseases of Jeanne. Infirmities, loneliness of my mother.

— Do your duty every day & trust God, for the next day.

— The only way to earn money is to work in a disinterested manner.

— An abridged wisdom. Grooming, prayer, work.

— Prayer: charity, wisdom, strength.

— Without charity, I am only but a tintinnabulating cymbal.

— My humiliations have been but blessings from God.

— Is my phase of egoism finished?

— The faculty of responding to the necessity of each minute, exactitude, in a word, must infallibly find its reward.

"The misfortune which is perpetuated produces on the soul the effect of old age upon the body; one can no longer move; one goes to bed...

On the other hand, one derives from extreme youth reasons for procrastination; when one has plenty of time to squander, one is persuaded that one can wait years before gambling on events."

CHATEAUBRIAND

93 B

HYGIENE · CONDUCT · METHOD

(Extracts from Emerson's *The Conduct of Life*)

Great men... have not been boasters and buffoons, but perceivers of *the terror of life*, and have manned themselves to face it.

"Fate is nothing but the deeds committed in a prior state of existence."

"What we wish for in youth, comes in heaps on us in old age," too often cursed with the granting of our prayer: and hence the high caution, that since we are sure of having what we wish we beware to ask only for high things.

The one prudence in life is concentration; the one evil is dissipation.

The poet Campbell said that "a man accustomed to work was equal to any achievement he resolved on, and that, for himself necessity, not inspiration, was the prompter of his muse."

In our daily affairs a decision must be made, — the best, if you can; but any is better than none.

The second substitute for temperament is drill, the power of use and routine.

"More are made good by exercitation than by nature," said Democritus.

Mirabeau said: "Why should we feel ourselves to be men, unless it be to succeed in everything, everywhere. You must say of nothing: *That is beneath me*, nor feel that anything can be out of your power. Nothing is impossible to the man who can will. *Is that necessary? That shall be*. This is the only *Law of success*."

We acquire the strength we have overcome.

The hero is he who is immovably centred.

The main difference between people seems to be, that one man can come under obligations on which you can rely;

and another is not. *As he has not a law within him, there's nothing to tie him to.*

If you would be powerful, pretend to be powerful.

Seeketh though great things? seek them not.

Conduct of Life

— Great men have not been [...] for high things.

— His heart (was) the throne of will.

— Life is search after power.

— No honest seeking goes unrewarded.

— We must reckon success a constitutional trait.

— The one prudence [...] of his muse.

— A decision [...] said Democritus.

— *Pecunia alter sanguis.*

— Mirabeau said [...] immovably centred.

— Your theories and plans of life are fair and commendable; — but will you stick?

— If you [...] powerful.

90
PRECIOUS NOTES

Do every day what duty and prudence want.
If you work every day, life will be more bearable.
Work *six* days without relent.

To find subjects, γνῶθι σεαυτόν ... (List of my tastes.)

Always be a poet, even in prose. Grand style (nothing is more beautiful than the commonplace).

First begin, and then make use of logic & analysis. Every hypothesis wants its conclusion.

Find the daily frenzy.

[THOUGHTS & APHORISMS]

[1]

Among the rights of which we have spoken in recent times, there is one that has been forgotten, which the demonstration of *all the world* is interested in, — the right to contradict one another.

[2]

There are three, to my knowledge, who have adopted this austere motto: Jean-Jacques, Louis Blanc, & George Sand. Joseph de Maistre says somewhere (in the *Considerations on France*, I believe): "If a writer adopts for a motto: *Vitam impendere vero*, there is much to wager that he is a liar."

[3]

Is it not true, my dear Gardet, that red is in itself a pleasurable choice, in that it transforms and exaggerates nature, but also because it obliges us to kiss ladies elsewhere than on the face? — I am sure not to displease you, my friend, who, like me, think that we must never lack dignity, except with the bitch of our heart.

Ch. Baudelaire

[4]

Every revolution has as its corollary the massacre of innocents.

[5]

When a merchant is not a felon, he is a savage.

[6]

Pederasty is the sole link that binds the magistracy to humanity.

[7]

Stoicism is a religion that has only one sacrament: *suicide*.

[8]

Sobriety is the mother of delectation: it is the support and *the counsel*.

[9]

A cat is a sweet vampire.

[10]

The absurd is the grace of people who are tired.

[11]

If Jesus Christ were to descend a second time on earth, M. Frank-Carré would say: he is a recidivate.

[12]

If we farted on About's nose, he would take this for an idea.

[13]

If religion disappeared from the world, it would be rediscovered in the heart of an atheist.

[14]

Nothing makes me understand the inanity of virtue better than La Madelène.

[15]

Learning is contradictory — there is a degree of consequence that is only within the reach of falsehood (Custine) — a sentence admired by Bodler.

NOVELLAS & NOVELS

A Hungry Man. — The Almanac. — The Love of Red. — *Love Parricide*. — Altar of the Will. — *The Automaton*. — Jeanne and the Automaton. — The Bathtub. — The Bath & Grooming. — *The Boa*. — *Boniface*. — The Triumph of Young Boniface. — *A Black Sheep*. — The Catechism of the Beloved Woman. — Crime at the College. — Icelandic Hemlock (see Gœrres). — *The Deserter*. — The Incorrigible Deserter. — The Undressing. — Early Childhood. — The Teachings of a Monster. — The Caretaker. — The Dishonest Woman. — *The End of the World*. — *The Reasonable Fool and the Beautiful Adventurer*. — The Happy of the [or some] World. — A Lottery Man. — The Involuntary Holocaust. — *The Holocaust*. — The Infamous Beloved. — *The Unicorn*. — *The Mistress of the Idiot*. — *The Virgin Mistress*. — The Husband Counter. — The Invisible Marquis (*very important*). — The Miners. — The Underwater World. — The Monsters. — The Negress with Blue Eyes. — The Father who is Always Waiting. — Heads or Tails.[6] — *The Fatal Portrait*. — The Impossible Portrait (because of antipathy). — The Malagasy Pretender. — *A Grudge*. — A Satisfied Grudge. — Dream Warning. — *The Dream Prophet*. — The Happy Repartee.

---

6. On a note, the titles "Heads or Tails" & "A Hungry Man" are united by a bracket in front of which one reads: Conspiracy.

— A Blow of Wind. — Speculation on Mail. — *The Trait of Whites*. — The Tribades. — *The Triumph of Jeanne*. — The Glassmakers. — A City in a City. — The Ingenuous Face.

[NOTES]

The Poor Hungry Man. Suppose a poor hungry man wants to profit from a public feast & a distribution of provisions so as to eat. He is beaten & clobbered by the multitude.

The Almanac. — Construct a speculation on a calculation of probabilities with respect to registered letters that do not arrive and the resulting indemnities.

The Love Parricide. — Picture of the inn. The wife, the husband, the father of the husband. The lovers, the whole city, including the imperial prosecutor and the gendarmes.

Reason for the wife's hatred of the father.

Jealousy of the husband. Murder, trial, execution.

The Automaton. — What he is, as a lover.

A sorcerer, in anticipating misfortune, wants to fight the laws of nature. His will: "If you truly love me…" And he returns automatically. His mistress wonders to herself which of the two existences is a dream. The automaton, whispered through the soul, persuades him that he was dreaming previously & that now he is really alive.

However, the soul, blushing to create happiness through lying, prefers committing a homicide and awakens his friend through death, to tell him of everything in paradise.

What is paradise?

Jeanne and the Automaton.

Old procurer. — All libertinage.

The grammatical dance.

The voice of the adjective penetrated me to the bone.

FRAGMENTS & NOTES

A. is a libertine.

A. is not yet.

A. dead is no more.

A. becomes a libertine.

The cold wife becomes the hot lover of a dead man.

Undoubtedly, in a few delirious moments, I lavished him with very lively caresses, for he told me several times that he would never have reckoned of so many diabolical errors in an honest woman's love, especially for a philosopher.

Voice of paradise.

The rub, it's the drama of Revelation.

The style is all the more decent when the ideas are less decent.

That which becomes the mysterious touch.

There is in thinness an indecency that renders her charming.

The end of the world. — A novel about *the last men.* — The same vices as previously. — Great distances. — Of war, of marriages, of politics among the last men.

The final palpitations of the world, struggles, rivalries. Hate. The taste for destruction & property. Love, in the decrepitude of humanity. Each sovereign has only fifty armed men. (Avoid [Grainville's] *The Last Man.*)

The Reasonable Fool and the Beautiful Adventurer. — Sensual rapture in the society of debauchees.

What horror and what rapture in love for a female spy, a female thief, etc. …! The moral reason for this rapture.

We must always return to de Sade, that is, to *the natural man*, to explain evil. Begin with a conversation, on love, between difficult people.

Monstrous feelings of friendship or admiration for a vicious woman.

Find horrific, strange adventures, through the capitals. *The Beautiful Adventurer*. — Novel rather than poem.

The Virgin Mistress. — The woman you do not ravish is the one that you love.

Æsthetic delicacy, idolatrous homage to the blasé.

That which makes the mistress more expensive is debauchery with other women. That which she loses in sensual pleasures, she gains in adoration. The consciousness of needing forgiveness renders man more lovable. Of chastity in love.

Heads or Tails. — Have discovered a conspiracy. — It's almost a creation. — It's a novel of which I have the denouement. — I dispose of the Empire. — Alternative, hesitation. — Why save the Empire? — Why destroy it? — *So* heads or tails.

MAYBE A COMEDY.

The Fatal Portrait. — Analytical method for verifying the miracle. Portrait of the deceased. Discovery of the will. Painting of a family marked with fatal sadness.

The Malagasy Pretender. — Find an issue of *Monde Illustré*. — See Mr. Reynaud, Pothey, & Delvau, 9 rue Veron.

The man who believes that his dog or his cat is the devil, or some imprisoned spirit.
The man who sees in his mistress a defect, an imaginary vice (physical?). Obsession.
The man who thinks himself ugly, or who sees in himself an imaginary vice (physical?). Obsession.
The man despairing of not being as handsome as his wife.
He who is not beautiful cannot enjoy love.

See the question of Sultana Alida.
The Decorations Fair. — Gazette of the Courts, September 30, 1858, Mr. Ducreux, substitute.

Series of scenes from the Directory & from the Consulate.
Modes of those eras.
Indecent prints from those eras.

The style of Montesquieu.

The raptures of the Church. Libertine impressions felt in Saint-Paul.

A little old woman that we follow.

The gallery of statues or paintings for the new Don Juan.

Theory of faith.

To apply to joy, to *the sensation of living*, the idea of the hyperacuity of the senses, applied by Poe to pain. To effect a creation through the pure logic of the contrary. The path is already traced out, against nature.

No remorse or regrets.
What does it matter to suffer much, when one has enjoyed much?
It is a law, a balance.
Find the moral algebra of this saying.
Various refrains.

Write to Malassis, to ask him for books on chauffeurs, robbers, sorcerers, especially after the revolutionary era.
Vendée.
Schinderhannes.
Robbers.
Witchcraft.
Sequestrations.
Palaces & prisons (underground).
And tortures & torments!

Everything young: petticoats, silk, perfumes, the knees of women.

The love of perfection. Everything that he detests, he destroys.

He finds an excuse.

Find the denouement by way of analysis.

Penetrate the sense (vague and general) of colors.

Divisions and subdivisions.

The voluptuary, having oscillated for a long time, is drawn by the ferocity in charity. What kind of misfortune can effect his conversion? The illness of his old accomplice. Struggle between egoism, pity, and remorse. His mistress (who has become his gal) makes him experience feelings of paternity. — Remorse: — who knows if he is not the author of some evil?

On the scrapbook of Philoxène Boyer.[7]

Among the rights of which we have spoken in recent times, there is one that has been forgotten, which the demonstration of *all the world* is interested in, — the right to contradict one another.

The drunkard. — Do not forget that intoxication is the negation of time, like every violent state of the spirit, & that, consequently, all the results of the loss of time must pass

---

7. *L'Echo de Paris* (19 juillet 1890).

before the eyes of the drunkard, without destroying in him the habit of returning to the morrow to his conversion, until the complete perversion of all feelings & the final catastrophe.

Biblical Sortilege. — The drunkard spying on and studying the drunkard.

The perfect man: the supreme of the appropriate, the caravan, the sentinel.

Of the power of the philter & magic in love as well as the evil eye.

Divine essence of the vicious circle (Flares).

THE PHILOSOPHER OWL

— That the title be set high, that the paper look full.

— That all the characters used should be of the same family, — typographical unity, — that the announcements should be close together, well aligned, of a uniform character.

— I am not very much partial to the habit of printing certain articles with a finer character than others.

— I have no idea about the suitability of dividing the page into three columns instead of dividing it into two.

— ARTICLES TO DO: General appreciation of the works of Th. Gautier, of Sainte-Beuve. — Appreciation of the direction & tendencies of the *Revue des Deux-Mondes*. — *Balzac, dramatic author.* — *Life of Dressing Rooms.* — *The Spirit of the Studio.* — *Gustave Planche*, radical exhaustion, nullity and cruelty of impotence, style of the imbecile and the magistrate. — Jules Janin: absolute exhaustion; no knowledge, no style, no good feelings. — *Alexandre Dumas*: to be entrusted to Monselet; nature of a farceur: to identify all the denials made by him of history and nature; style of a banterer. — *Eugene Sue*: stupid and counterfeit talent. — Paul Feval: idiot.

— WORKS OF WHICH WE CAN MAKE A VALUATION: The last volume of the *Causeries du lundi*. Poetry of Houssaye and Brizeux. *Lettres et Mélanges* of Joseph de Maistre. *La Religieuse de Toulouse*: TO KILL. The translation of Emerson. Make reports of artistic facts. To examine if the absence of certainty and the present tyranny enables us to discuss, with regard to art and the bookstore, the acts of the administration.

— To examine if the absence of certainty does not forbid us to take account of the works of history and religion. Avoid all visibly socialistic tendencies and allusions, and obviously courtieresque.

— We monitor and advise each other with complete frankness. Write out for us five a list of important persons, men of letters, editors of magazines and newspapers, friends in propaganda, reading rooms, circles, restaurants and cafes, booksellers to whom we must send *le Hibou philosophe*; make articles on some ancient authors, those who, having advanced their century, can give lessons for the regeneration of contemporary literature. Example: Mercier, Bernardin de Saint-Pierre, etc. ...

— Make an article on *Florian* (Monselet);

— on *Sedaine* (Monselet or Champfleury);

— on *Ourliac* (Champfleury);

the five of us to make a long article: *The Sale of Old Words at the Auction*, of the *Classical School*, of the *School of Classical Chivalry*, of the *Nascent Romantic School*, of the *Lunatic School*, of the *School of the Lance of Toledo*, of the *Olympian School* (V. Hugo), of the *Plastic School* (T. Gautier), of the *Pagan School* (1) (Banville), of the *Phthisic School*, of the *School of Good Sense* (2), of the *Farcical-Melancholico School* (Alfred de Musset).

— As for the novellas that we shall produce, that they belong to so-called *fantastic* literature, or that they are studies of mores, scenes of real life, as far as possible in a bare style, true and full of sincerity.

DRAWINGS

Nº 30

"Arm. Barthet."

Drawing in pencil on a page of Nadar's drawings of Jongkind & Clésinger.
22.2 × 17.5 cm. Around 1850.

BNF, Est. Phot., res.

№ 31
[August Blanqui & other drawings.]
Pen & India ink. 27.5 × 18.5 cm. 1849–1850.
Private Collection, Paris.

Nº 28
[Charles Asselineau.]
Pen & India ink. 12×13 cm, in *Le Petit Figaro*. 1849–1850,
according to Maurice Tourneux. Original missing.

№ 25
Heavenly Vision for the use of Paul Chenavard.
Pen & vermilion. 19.9 × 12.9 cm. From the mid-1850s.
Bibliothèque littéraire Jacques Doucet, Paris.

DRAWINGS

Nº 21
La Fanfarlo.
Crayon. 19.6 × 15.3 cm. Date of composition unknown.
Dina Vierny Foundation.

DRAWINGS

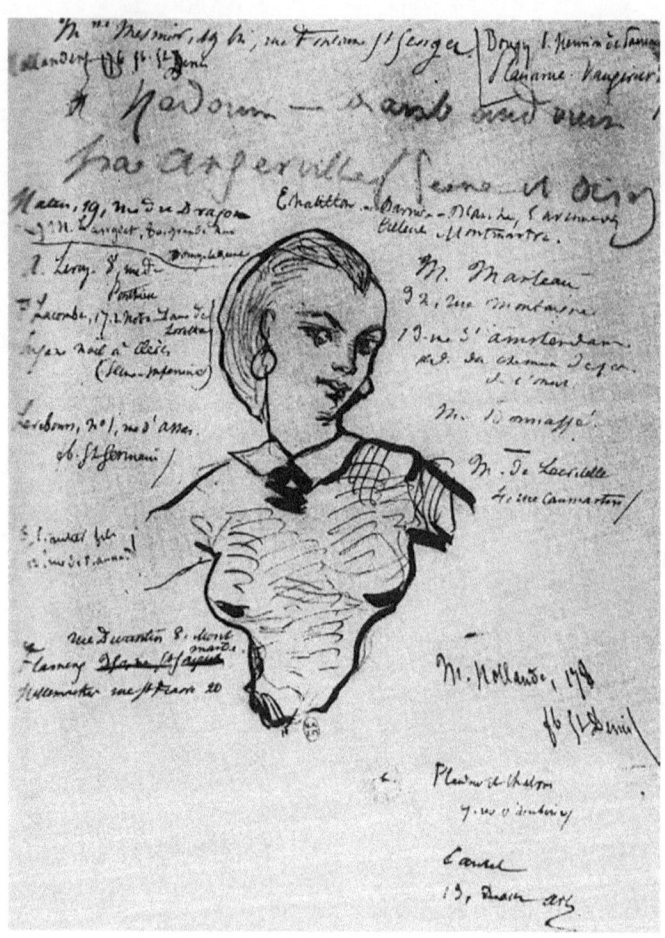

Nº 13
[Portrait of Jeanne Duval annotated by Poulet-Malassis.]
Pen & India ink. 25.6 × 19.3 cm. 1858–1860.
Dina Vierny Foundation.

DRAWINGS

№ 14
[Portrait of Jeanne Duval.]
Pen & India ink. 20.6 × 14.5 cm. 1865.
Musée d'Orsay.

№ 15
[Portrait said to be of Jeanne Duval.]
Pen & India ink. 15 × 15 cm. Date of composition unknown.
Collection Christian Bernadac.

Félix Nadar, [caricature of Baudelaire.] 1859–60.

DRAWINGS

Nº 2
[Baudelaire by himself under the influence of hashish.]
Pen & stump, enhanced with vermillion. 21.5 × 17 cm. 1842–1845.
Private collection.

Alfred Briend, *Baudelaire by himself under the influence of hashish*.
Etching. 1842–1845.

Nº 12
[Self-portrait.]
Pen, India ink, & red pencil. 17.6 × 10 cm. 1863–1864.
Musée d'Orsay.

DRAWINGS

[Self-portrait with other drawings.]
1845–1847.
Cite de l'Architecture.

DRAWINGS

Nº 10

[Self-portrait.]

Pen & red pencil. 20.4 × 12 cm. Around 1860.

Collection Spœlberch de Lovenjoul, bibliothèque de l'Institut de France.

DRAWINGS

Nº 9
[Self-portrait.]
Pen & red pencil. 21.9 × 15.2 cm. Around 1860.
Musée d'Orsay.

№ 8
[Self-portrait.]
Pen. 19.5 × 15.1 cm. Around 1857–1858.
Private Collection.

Étienne Carjat, Portrait of Baudelaire. C. 1862.

A NOTE ON THIS EDITION

Although this edition has an introduction, it has no critical appendix, making it more like discovering Baudelaire's notebook itself, as naked as he wished to be in *Mon cœur mis à nu*. The work of interpretation and discovery is left then to each reader. What follow are some brief notes concerning the origin of the texts translated herein.

Choice of Consoling Maxims on Love: Originally published in *Le Corsaire-Satan* (March 3, 1846). Article signed "Baudelaire-Dufaÿs." Taken from Baudelaire's *Œuvres posthumes*, 3rd ed. (Mercure de France, 1908). Hereafter cited as OP III.

Autobiographical Note: Taken from OP III. Included as a preface to what editors named the "Journaux intimes" (Intimate Journals), which included *Fusées & Mon cœur mis à nu*. The title "Journaux intimes" is not Baudelaire's; therefore, it has not been retained.

Flares *& My Heart Laid Bare*: The translations of *Fusées & Mon cœur mis à nu* are based on André Guyaux's revision of the Crepit-Blin edition of Baudelaire's manuscripts. Our numbering for both works follows that of Guyaux, who departs from Malassis regarding §§ 86 *&* 88 of *Mon cœur*..., which have also been placed at the end of *Fusées*. As he explains, certain texts from *Mon cœur*... overlap with *Fusées* in their also being statements of reflexive counsel. Hence the leap in numbering from 22 to 86 — nothing has been left untranslated, and nothing is missing. Baudelaire left no definitive edition of either work, but §§ 86–93 of HYGIENE... could very likely be part of *Fusées*.

Novellas & Novels: Taken from OP III & listed under the section "Projects & Notes."

Fragments: Taken from OP III & listed under the section "Variety."

Notes: Taken from OP III and listed under the section "Theater." This brief series of notes were appended by the editors of OP III to the end of the chapter "The Drunkard," a letter (Saturday, January 28, 1854) to J.-H. Weaving in which Baudelaire discusses in detail a projected play he referred to as a "lamentable nightmare." The main character was to be a common worker (a sawyer) & idle dreamer with aspirations beyond his status. The play would be replete with misery, unemployment, quarrels, drunkenness, jealousy, and eventually murder. Poetic songs recited in a *goguette* would, Baudelaire said, "show the lyrical, often comic and awkward instincts of the people."

The Philosopher Owl: The title of a weekly that had been conceived by Baschet, Baudelaire, Champfleury, Monselet, and André Thomas around 1853. Taken from OP III and listed under the section "Baudelaire Journalist." Originally published by Octave Uzanne in *Le Livre* (10 septembre 1884).

In Flares and My Heart Laid Bare, letters or words crossed out by Baudelaire have been set between square brackets [ ]; letters or words added by him between ‹ ›. Any words set as such ‹[ ]› were added then deleted by Baudelaire. In the case of two consecutive words, with the first in square brackets and the second between square or ‹ ›, the second word or phrase replaces the first. Baudelaire's capitalization, as his orthography in general, has been respected, even if at odds with contemporary practice. The aim here was not to *contemporize* CB, *Satan forbid*, but to create a translation as close to mid-19th century English as possible. Hence, i.e., for Baudelaire's "porte-voix," the choice of "speaking-trumpet," which is the corresponding phrase of the period. Other translators have rendered "porte-voix" as "megaphone," but that word dates to 1878 (possibly coined by Th. Edison), thus it postdates CB's text by a good number of years.

For copies of CB's original manuscripts, see Eugène Crépet's edition of CB's *Œuvres posthumes* (Quantin, 1887), Philippe Soupault's *Baudelaire* (Rieder, 1931), & tome II of *Œuvres complètes* (Le Club du Meilleur Livre, 1955).

COLOPHON

MY HEART LAID BARE

was handset in InDesign CC.

The text & page numbers are set in *Adobe Jenson Pro*.
The titles are set in *Quasimoda*.

Book design & typesetting: Alessandro Segalini
Cover design: Rainer J. Hanshe & Alessandro Segalini
Cover image credit: Daumier, *Riot Scene*, ca. 1871 (M. 168).
Pen & black ink with grey wash, 160 × 260 mm. Paris, private collection.

MY HEART LAID BARE

is published by Contra Mundum Press.

CONTRA MUNDUM PRESS

Dedicated to the value & the indispensable importance of the individual voice, to works that test the boundaries of thought & experience.

The primary aim of Contra Mundum is to publish translations of writers who in their use of form and style are *à rebours*, or who deviate significantly from more programmatic & spurious forms of experimentation. Such writing attests to the volatile nature of modernism. Our preference is for works that have not yet been translated into English, are out of print, or are poorly translated, for writers whose thinking & æsthetics are in opposition to timely or mainstream currents of thought, value systems, or moralities. We also reprint obscure and out-of-print works we consider significant but which have been forgotten, neglected, or overshadowed.

There are many works of fundamental significance to Weltliteratur (& Weltkultur) that still remain in relative oblivion, works that alter and disrupt standard circuits of thought — these warrant being encountered by the world at large. It is our aim to render them more visible.

For the complete list of forthcoming publications, please visit our website. To be added to our mailing list, send your name and email address to: info@contramundum.net

Contra Mundum Press
P.O. Box 1326
New York, NY 10276
USA

OTHER CONTRA MUNDUM PRESS TITLES

2012 *Gilgamesh*
      Ghérasim Luca, *Self-Shadowing Prey*
      Rainer J. Hanshe, *The Abdication*
      Walter Jackson Bate, *Negative Capability*
      Miklós Szentkuthy, *Marginalia on Casanova*
      Fernando Pessoa, *Philosophical Essays*
2013 Elio Petri, *Writings on Cinema & Life*
      Friedrich Nietzsche, *The Greek Music Drama*
      Richard Foreman, *Plays with Films*
      Louis-Auguste Blanqui, *Eternity by the Stars*
      Miklós Szentkuthy, *Towards the One & Only Metaphor*
      Josef Winkler, *When the Time Comes*
2014 William Wordsworth, *Fragments*
      Josef Winkler, *Natura Morta*
      Fernando Pessoa, *The Transformation Book*
      Emilio Villa, *The Selected Poetry of Emilio Villa*
      Robert Kelly, *A Voice Full of Cities*
      Pier Paolo Pasolini, *The Divine Mimesis*
      Miklós Szentkuthy, *Prae, Vol. 1*
2015 Federico Fellini, *Making a Film*
      Robert Musil, *Thought Flights*
      Sándor Tar, *Our Street*
      Lorand Gaspar, *Earth Absolute*
      Josef Winkler, *The Graveyard of Bitter Oranges*
      Ferit Edgü, *Noone*
      Jean-Jacques Rousseau, *Narcissus*
      Ahmad Shamlu, *Born Upon the Dark Spear*

2016　Jean-Luc Godard, *Phrases*
　　　　Otto Dix, *Letters, Vol. 1*
　　　　Maura Del Serra, *Ladder of Oaths*
　　　　Pierre Senges, *The Major Refutation*

SOME FORTHCOMING TITLES

Rainer J. Hanshe, *Shattering the Muses*
Pierre Senges, *Ahab*

THE FUTURE OF KULCHUR
A PATRONAGE PROJECT

LEND CONTRA MUNDUM PRESS (CMP) YOUR SUPPORT

With bookstores and presses around the world struggling to survive, and many actually closing, we are forming this patronage project as a means for establishing a continuous & stable foundation to safeguard our longevity. Through this patronage project we would be able to remain free of having to rely upon government support &/or other official funding bodies, not to speak of their timelines & impositions. It would also free CMP from suffering the vagaries of the publishing industry, as well as the risk of submitting to commercial pressures in order to persist, thereby potentially compromising the integrity of our catalog.

CAN YOU SACRIFICE $10 A WEEK FOR KULCHUR?

For the equivalent of merely 2–3 coffees a week, you can help sustain CMP and contribute to the future of kulchur. To participate in our patronage program we are asking individuals to donate $500 per year, which amounts to $42/month, or $10/week. Larger donations are of course welcome and beneficial. All donations are tax-deductible through our fiscal sponsor Fractured Atlas. If preferred, donations can be made in two installments. We are seeking a minimum of 300 patrons per year and would like for them to commit to giving the above amount for a period of three years.

WHAT WE OFFER

Part tax-deductible donation, part exchange, for your contribution you will receive every CMP book published during the patronage period as well as 20 books from our back catalog. When possible, signed or limited editions of books will be offered as well.

WHAT WILL CMP DO WITH YOUR CONTRIBUTIONS?

Your contribution will help with basic general operating expenses, yearly production expenses (book printing, warehouse & catalog fees, etc.), advertising & outreach, and editorial, proofreading, translation, typography, design and copyright fees. Funds may also be used for participating in book fairs and staging events. Additionally, we hope to rebuild the *Hyperion* section of the website in order to modernize it.

From Pericles to Mæcenas & the Renaissance patrons, it is the magnanimity of such individuals that have helped the arts to flourish. Be a part of helping your kulchur flourish; be a part of history.

HOW

To lend your support & become a patron, please visit the subscription page of our website: contramundum.net/subscription

For any questions, write us at: info@contramundum.net

www.ingramcontent.com/pod-product-compliance
Lightning Source LLC
Chambersburg PA
CBHW031314160426
43196CB00007B/532